# THE GOLDEN TELESCOPE

## A GUIDE TO DISCOVERING HARMONY AND FINANCIAL WELLBEING FOR OWNER-MANAGERS AND PROFESSIONALS

**DOUG McLARTY & ROSS McSHANE**

www.goldentelescope.ca

great river media inc.

*The Golden Telescope*

Doug McLarty and Ross McShane

Great River Media

Library and Archives Canada Cataloguing in Publication

McLarty, Doug & McShane, Ross – Authors.
The Golden Telescope/Doug McLarty & Ross McShane

ISBN 978-0-9868242-3-4

Great River Media
250 City Centre Drive, Suite 500
Ottawa, ON. Canada
K1R 6K7

For inquiries about the book or to contact the authors, visit:
www.goldentelescope.ca

Text design: Carole McLachlin Design
Cover design: Aerographics
Printed and bound in Canada

PRINTED ON
RECYCLED PAPER

# NOTICE TO READER

This book contains a high-level analysis of the financial circumstances of fictional characters. These characters are based on real client situations, but the recommendations are not appropriate for everyone. Your circumstances may be different. Before making any significant decisions, a detailed analysis of your specific circumstances is required.

# PRAISE FOR THE
# GOLDEN TELESCOPE

"This is a great book. It is concise, enjoyable, easy to read and provides lots of pertinent and practical advice for those of us with limited financial knowledge. It reminds the reader of the importance of having a solid financial plan and of the benefits of having a team of financial professionals working for you. Highly recommended!"

**WENDY PULLAN**, MD

"This is a must-read book unless you want to find yourself without the knowledge and tools that can prevent financial hardship. I believe that to ignore *The Golden Telescope's* six principles is a guarantee of harsh financial surprises. I have followed every principle outlined in the book with great success. Protect yourself, your business, and most importantly, your family. Doug and Ross have done that and more for mine."

**BARRY DWORKIN**, MD, CFRA RADIO HOST

"Too often financial advice is dispensed generically. But professionals and business owners have unique needs that call for unique solutions — as Doug McLarty and Ross McShane deftly show in this book. Topics covered include insurance, taxation, investing and succession planning — all knitted together in an engaging and easy-to-read way."

**LARRY MACDONALD**, INVESTMENT COLUMNIST FOR CANADIAN BUSINESS AND THE GLOBE AND MAIL

"Be sure to read this book if you would like to understand some straightforward approaches to complicated tax, insurance, financial and succession planning issues that business owners need to deal with — but often put off because the task seems too daunting. You will finish *The Golden Telescope* with a clear understanding of what you need to do."

**TOM DONNELLY**, PRESIDENT OF DONNELLY AUTOMOTIVE GROUP, FORMER CHAIR OF THE CANADIAN AUTOMOBILE DEALERS ASSOCIATION

"*The Golden Telescope* emphasizes the importance of a financial plan that takes into account everything from complicated corporate structures to family goals. My family and I were aware of all of the implications of selling our business because we worked with professionals who helped us see the before and after big pictures."

**PAUL BELISLE**, FORMER OWNER OF BELISLE AUTOMOBILES

# PROLOGUE

On the eighteenth green of the Whispering Willows Country Club, Gary stood carefully over a ball sitting five feet from the hole.

He took a practice swing, then reached his putter back, tapped the ball gently and watched it roll by the cup an inch to the left, coming to a rest two feet past the hole.

"And with that," said Mike, "victory is mine."

Gary grunted.

"What's going on with your putting these days?" asked Mike, as Gary tapped the ball into the hole with one hand to complete his round. "You're getting worse as you get older."

Gary forced a smile. He didn't like when Mike joked about their age difference. Gary was 58 years old and on top of the world, the owner of a successful car dealership and the vice-chair of the local chamber of commerce. The only thing he had in common with Mike, a 42-year-old freelance IT consultant, was that they were evenly matched at golf. But now Mike had won the last five times they had played.

"I just can't seem to make the easy ones these days," said Gary. "It's driving me crazy."

The two men walked toward the clubhouse.

"Let's come out early next time and we can spend some time on the practice green," said Mike. "I can give you some pointers."

"Sure," said Gary, unenthusiastically.

"Unless it's not something physical," said Mike. "Are you

distracted? Guilty conscience? Something else on your mind?"

Gary chuckled. "Do you have time for a quick one?" he asked.

"Sure," said Mike. "Sandra's working late at the hospital, so I'm making dinner for the kids. But I've got half an hour."

They ordered drinks and sat down at a table in the member's lounge. Mike yawned.

"Do you need a nap?" asked Gary.

"I was up late with Katie, helping her work on her astronomy badge for Girl Guides," said Mike. "We must have spent two hours trying to find Polaris."

"What the heck is Polaris?" said Gary.

"It's the north star, Gary. It's part of the constellation Ursa Minor, also known as the Little Bear. Didn't you know that?"

"I know about the Golden Bear. Jack Nicklaus, right?"

Mike smiled. "I didn't know about Polaris until yesterday. I don't really even understand how to work a telescope."

"I guess you're only good with modern technology," said Gary. "Anyway, not to change the subject…"

Here we go, Mike thought to himself. He had been teasing Gary but now, it seemed, he was about to hear the psychological issues causing his friend's putting problems.

"I'm feeling all this pressure on me from everyone," Gary continued.

"Like what?" said Mike. "I thought business was good."

"Business is great," said Gary. "But now that we've got this place in Florida, Jennifer wants to be there more often. She thinks I should spend less time at work."

"There's a problem I'd like to have."

"But the kids aren't ready to take over. They keep asking for more responsibility, but they just haven't learned the business well enough yet."

"You're irreplaceable," said Mike.

"And," Gary paused.

"And what?"

"I made some bad stock picks."

"Well, there are always ups and downs on the market, right? It's a long game."

"Right. But these were unusually big downs."

"Like how big?"

"My portfolio went from $1.2 million to $700,000 in a year and a half."

"Wow," said Mike. "You've got a real knack. You should write a blog about investing."

"I was on a roll for a while," said Gary. "Got a few good tips and was up 12 per cent. But then I had a run of bad luck."

"Why are you managing your own stock portfolio?" asked Mike. "You really have time for that?"

"Sure. Why not? You know Tim Donaldson?"

"The high school teacher?"

"Yeah. He told me about this investment strategy that he said couldn't miss. He had made something like 10 per cent a year for the past four years, while the market was bouncing up and down."

"But just because he did okay for a while doesn't prove anything. Maybe he was just lucky."

"I don't want to be one of those losers who get single-digit returns," said Gary. "Might as well put your money in a savings account."

"Single-digit returns are pretty boring," said Mike, "compared to blowing half of a million on day trades."

"Listen, don't repeat this to anyone. Don't even tell Sandra. Jennifer doesn't know and I'd rather she didn't find out. I don't want her to worry."

"You don't want her to worry, or you don't want to have to explain why you lost an amount of money equivalent to the price of a small airplane?"

Gary ignored the question. "I suppose you guys don't have any money concerns at all," he said.

"I don't," said Mike. "But Sandra does. She makes a killing but she still acts like we're still in university scraping together our cash from part-time jobs."

"It could be worse," said Gary. He was trying to stop thinking about his investment portfolio, but it kept popping back into his mind.

"But we don't have to live like that anymore," said Mike. "We've been talking for years about buying a cottage, but she says we can't afford it. It's ridiculous. How can we not afford it? Our neighbours bought a summer home last year. A summer home! The wife doesn't even work."

"Is she not keeping you in the manner to which you've become accustomed? I'll call her and tell her to buy you some flowers and a box of chocolates, maybe take you out for a nice meal or send you for a day at the spa."

"It's not just about me," said Mike. "I want the kids to be able to enjoy the cottage while they're still young. There's no point when they're teenagers. You wouldn't believe what she makes, but she doesn't think it's enough."

Gary had a rough idea of what radiologists earned. One or two of them had filled out credit applications to buy high-end vehicles at his dealership and it briefly made him wish he had listened to his mother's advice about medical school.

"You should have more than enough money to buy a cottage," Gary said. "Just do some of the math for her, walk through it together and she'll see."

"It's not that simple," said Mike. Gary didn't understand what it was like talking to Sandra about money. "Anyway, it's not the end of the world. I'm sure once we get a bit further ahead, she'll feel a bit more comfortable. I just want to make sure she and the kids get to enjoy life now and not just some day in the future."

"That's what Jennifer has been saying to me about spending more time in Florida," said Gary. "We should be enjoying ourselves now."

"I'll tell you what," said Mike. "Why don't we have Jennifer talk to Sandra? It might not solve your problem, but it could help fix mine."

# INTRODUCTION

We meet couples like Gary and Jennifer and Mike and Sandra all the time — people who are successful professionally, but struggling with family decisions about cottages and private schools, plus financial matters like investments and insurance. As business owners and professionals, they're juggling a set of competing objectives and complex circumstances, trying to balance immediate family needs with the long-term goal of financial security and retirement.

Look at Gary. He's successful in business, and together with Jennifer, has a wonderful family. He's earning a great living — more than $400,000 per year. He started a car dealership 20 years ago and he's worked hard to build it into a business that is now worth several million dollars.

Gary and Jennifer have four kids aged 17 to 31, two of whom are working in the car dealership with him. He's a few years away from retirement, and he and his wife have the capacity to achieve many of the dreams they've been working toward for years.

But Gary isn't making long-term financial decisions based on his unique circumstances as a business owner and the specific goals he has for himself and his family. He's not working with a comprehensive financial plan. And he's not relying on trusted advisers to assist him in the process. Instead, he's acting on whims, like picking stocks based on something he reads in the newspaper, sees on TV or hears from a friend. He's making a lot of decisions on his own, often without good advice. And in some cases he acts on bad advice, whether that comes from a friend, a colleague, or someone in the financial services sector who's trying to sell him something. He's like someone trying to lose weight based on the latest fad diet that he read about in a magazine.

Sandra, meanwhile, has a different set of concerns. As Gary guessed, she earns a lot of money, about $550,000 a year, as a radiologist. But as her husband Mike pointed out, despite her significant income, Sandra faces a lot of competing pressures that cause her to worry about having enough money for both today and the future. She wants to give her kids the best possible start in life, meaning she and Mike are considering private school, not to mention other expenses like family vacations, summer camps, and extracurricular activities, many of which are not cheap. Sandra is also supporting her parents, who just moved to Canada from their home in India. In addition to her kids, and to some extent Mike, she now considers them her dependents as well.

And while she has a good job with lots of security, Sandra worries about saving for her future because she has no pension. With the health-care industry in flux, she's concerned about job security. There are no guarantees that she will always earn what she brings in now.

Sandra's anxieties lead her to take a fairly cautious approach to everything to do with money. Her investments tend to be very safe. She saves as much money as possible every year, shielding it in investments that are difficult to liquidate so that she and Mike aren't tempted to access them for home renovations, trips or other lifestyle expenses.

Although Gary and Sandra are fictional characters, we bet you can relate to one or both of them. As a professional or the owner of your own business, you juggle all the tasks of managing your career and your bottom line, plus all the other demands on your time and energy, including family.

You probably get tremendous satisfaction from your work. And one of your biggest motivations for working so hard is to ensure that you create as much value and income as you can for yourself, and especially for the people you love. Yet you probably spend most of your time building your business or practice and very little time figuring out how the proceeds of your hard work will help you achieve your long-term goals.

How would you answer the following questions?

- Have you figured out the best way to extract income from your business in a tax-efficient manner, so you're getting the most value from your hard work?
- Do you have a strategy to protect and expand your assets with the right balance between risk and reward? Have you determined how to achieve the appropriate level of return without exposing yourself to unreasonable risk?
- Do you have a plan to successfully transfer your business or the wealth you generate from it to your family when you stop working? Have you figured out what would happen if that day comes sooner than expected, in the event something happens to you before your planned retirement?

We're guessing you didn't answer yes to all of those questions. If that's the case, you're certainly not alone. Gary and Sandra would probably answer no to all of them. Like many other busy people, you've been focused on responding to all of the immediate demands that are placed on you. That doesn't leave much time for long-term planning.

Maybe you have a vague sense that it will all work out in the end. Someday, you'll organize things properly. Or maybe someone will come along and offer you a big cheque and take over what you've created. Then you and your family will ride off into the sunset and pursue all of your dreams.

But deep down inside, you know it's not that simple.

You want to structure your affairs properly. But the truth is that when it comes to researching, analyzing, and planning the best way to extract, protect, and increase the money you earn, you just don't have enough time left over after work and family commitments to be proactive, thoughtful, and comprehensive about your approach.

The answers aren't quick and easy, nor are they readily available from existing financial literature or the vast majority of financial advisers. Here's why:

## AS AN OWNER–MANAGER OR PROFESSIONAL, YOU HAVE UNIQUE REQUIREMENTS AND UNUSUAL RISKS THAT MOST FINANCIAL ADVISERS AND AUTHORS SIMPLY DON'T UNDERSTAND OR TAKE INTO ACCOUNT IN THEIR ADVICE TO YOU.

From years of working with clients just like you, we can tell you that owner-managers and professionals are exposed to a number of unique hazards and risks. These traps and dangers aren't addressed by the plethora of generic financial literature that you find at the bookstore, nor by the financial advisers at most banks and brokerages, because these issues aren't relevant to the majority of consumers, who are employees.

As an owner-manager or professional, your situation is remarkably different. So you have to move carefully and strategically to avoid making the wrong decisions. We've identified 12 pitfalls that are unique to people like Gary and Sandra, and you:

1. Thinking you are in the same situation as others who don't have your unique requirements.
2. Having an investment strategy that's like a fad diet: too aggressive, risky and unrealistic.
3. Stressing about your finances and looking up investment values daily.
4. Thinking you're diversified when you're really not.
5. Paying too much in fees, and paying fees that are not tax-deductible, therefore costing you extra money.
6. Having too much or the wrong kind of life insurance.
7. Paying too much in taxes because you're taking money out of your business the wrong way.
8. Relying on a cookie-cutter financial plan that's actually a sales

pitch to get you to invest or buy insurance or other financial products.

9.  Using a plan that doesn't take into account all the facets of your life and business and all the members of your family.
10. Thinking succession planning is a transaction you can work on when you're close to retirement.
11. Investing before reducing debt or borrowing unreasonable amounts to invest.
12. Being afraid to spend because you don't know where you stand. Believe it or not, you might actually be able to spend more than you think you can.

If you don't have a strategy to navigate all of these pitfalls, or rely on the wrong advice, you could be at risk of losing tens of thousands of dollars, if not more, over the next few years. You could be forced to retire a year or two later than you otherwise might, maybe even later than that. And you could be creating a much smaller nest egg for your family, despite all your hard work.

You know what's at stake. But we're guessing that because of your busy life and the complexity of your financial requirements, you haven't taken the time to sit down and create a comprehensive, customized, and detailed financial plan, or at least not one that addresses all of your needs. Perhaps the idea is daunting or even scary.

Certainly, research shows that 65 per cent of owner-managers and professionals have no plan at all. Of the remaining 35 per cent, our experience is that about 34 per cent have a plan that isn't thorough enough. Maybe they have something that was given to them from a financial service provider that looks like a plan, but it's really just a rationale for investing with that adviser. We'll address these cookie-cutter plans and explain why they are nowhere near what you need.

If you're in the remaining one per cent, congratulations and stop reading. You don't need this book.

But if you're in the vast majority, this book can help you. And it's not a long or tough read that feels like a homework assignment.

It's meant to be helpful, relatable, and interesting. There are no acronyms or charts and graphs. You won't have to learn a lot of new terminology.

The truth is that a lot of financial service providers don't understand your world and the tax complications that come with it. However, we do. Over the last 30 years, we've worked with thousands of business owners and professionals. At McLarty & Co, we think like entrepreneurs and professionals because we are entrepreneurs and professionals.

Our passion is helping owner-managers and professionals to realize the wealth that they've created with their hard work, and to avoid the many pitfalls of a financial service industry that doesn't cater to their needs and can often be counterproductive or leave them exposed to significant risks.

We can't tell you the number of times we've seen clients who have been set on the wrong path by people in the financial industry who don't understand their specific needs or — even worse — deliberately mislead them. And it's not just the sharks that you have to be wary of. Unfortunately, many people in the financial industry treat every customer the same way, even though the needs of owner-managers and professionals are very different from those of the typical customer. The cookie-cutter approach of many big banks, brokerages, and insurance companies not only doesn't work for people like you, it could actually be counterproductive and cost you thousands of dollars.

Frankly, we're tired of encountering business owners and professionals who are being given the wrong advice because their financial planner is acting in his or her best interests rather than theirs. It doesn't happen every time, but it does happen often enough that we want to warn everyone to be careful.

That's why we've written this book. Our goal is to make sure you don't become one of those clients.

# THE GOLDEN TELESCOPE

Sandra ordered a mineral water and glanced at her watch. As usual, she was a few minutes early. Maybe she could quickly scan the Internet on her phone and see if she could find out more about Katie's birthday present.

As she browsed a rather unhelpful website, Sandra's mind wandered to a conversation at the clinic earlier in the day. Her colleague Melanie had mentioned in passing that they were looking for someone to take some extra shifts on the weekend. Sandra hadn't said anything at the time, but she was thinking of offering to take some of the extra work. It wouldn't hurt to have a bit more income, especially if they were going to send Katie and Jake to private school.

Mike was right: she worried a lot about money. Well, to be more precise, she worried about their future. It wasn't really the cash, but the fear of not having enough of it so that everything would be okay.

But did she actually worry too much? Mike didn't seem to be troubled about these things at all. He was convinced that no matter what they spent their income on now — cottages, expensive trips, golf club memberships, private schools — everything would work out in the end.

Jennifer walked into the restaurant and Sandra started to turn off her phone. The two women didn't spend as much time together as their golfing-buddy husbands, but they met occasionally for coffee. Today Sandra was enlisting Jennifer's last-minute help as she scrambled to pull off a decent birthday party for Katie. Jennifer was one of those people who knew all the little details about event planning. With four older kids, she had also hosted many more birthday parties than Sandra had.

"Are you addicted to your email?" Jennifer asked, smiling at Sandra's phone. "I look at mine every two minutes."

"Actually, I was looking at telescope stuff," said Sandra. "For Katie."

"For Katie? She's turning nine, right?"

"Yep."

"And she's not into dolls and clothes?"

Sandra laughed. "A little bit. But she's really excited about astronomy. I thought it was just a phase at first. But she can't stop reading about it."

"So you're getting her a telescope. Wow, that's a very grown-up gift."

Sandra wondered if she was making Katie into a smaller version of herself: serious and academic rather than fun and light-hearted like Mike. A telescope did seem like a grown-up gift. But Mike thought it was a good idea too. She put that thought out of her mind.

"So I was thinking about the best location for the party," Jennifer was saying. "I know the owner of Tina's Turtles. They could probably fit something in. It's a little bit expensive but the kids really love seeing all the reptiles. Also, I know this woman who does cakes out of her own kitchen."

"That sounds great," said Sandra. She paused. "Jenn, can I ask you something?"

"Of course."

"Do you worry about money?"

"Sure, of course," said Jennifer. "Honestly, you have no idea. But look, if Tina's Turtles is too expensive, there are other options."

"Oh, it's not that," said Sandra. "Everything you've suggested for the party is fine. It's something else. Look, don't worry about it."

"Hey, we can talk about the party later. What's up? Is something wrong?"

"No, everything's good. It's just that I always worry that we're not going to have enough for all the things we want to do. And Mike never worries about it at all. I call him Happy-Go-Mikey. So I wonder if I'm worrying too much."

"So are you guys fighting about money?"

"No, we're not fighting. We're just not agreeing about what to do. We've been avoiding the subject, mostly. But we've been looking into private school for the kids and Mike wants to buy a cottage."

"Well, why not?"

"It's just that even though I'm earning way more money than I ever thought I would, I worry that it won't last forever."

"But you don't live extravagantly. You spend far less than we do on some things, believe me. You can afford some of this stuff without using all your savings, can't you?"

"I guess so, but I also feel like we should be paying off our mortgage before we do some of these other things. And with interest rates so low, it's like we have to save even more every year to be able to have enough money when we retire."

"Seriously, Sandra, I admire you for being so careful about everything. I wish Gary were that conservative with our cash. He thinks there's always going to be a bigger payday tomorrow. But I wouldn't think all of this would be an issue, given that you both have good jobs."

"It's not that simple," said Sandra. "My income goes into a corporation, and every time we take money out to pay for extra things, we have to pay tax on it. And I'm in the top tax bracket, so it's a big hit every time."

"That all sounds pretty complicated. Maybe you should talk to someone about it."

"Yeah, maybe you're right. Anyway, sorry to trouble you with that."

"No problem," said Jennifer. "So, you're okay with Tina's Turtles. Because we can also do this at that crappy bowling alley in the mall, you know. They make a mean hot dog, if you don't mind it being a few days old."

Sandra laughed as Jennifer continued. "And we can cut some

people from the invitation list. Tell Katie she's only allowed to invite one friend. Technically, that's still a party."

"Stop it!" said Sandra. "I can afford Tina's Turtles! Let's go all out!"

"Anyway," Jennifer said, "since you brought up the whole money thing, wait until you hear what I just found out."

As we said before, the needs of a professional like Sandra or an owner-manager like Gary are unique and complex. And as they have both discovered, many people they talk to about their financial goals don't understand that. And the books and articles available don't address their circumstances either. Here's what people like Sandra, Gary and you won't find in most of the generic financial literature that's currently available:

- Your financial planning requirements are dramatically different from those of other people you know who derive most of their income from regular employment.
- Most financial service providers will give you a cookie-cutter plan that isn't suited to the complexity of your situation and doesn't take into account your unique requirements as an owner-manager or professional.
- You probably don't have a financial plan, but even if you do, it's probably very one-dimensional and not anything close to the comprehensive, sophisticated plan you need.
- You can save time and money, reduce stress, and simplify your life through an integrated plan that doesn't leave you dealing with a series of diverse and distinct providers who never talk to each other.
- Most insurance and investment advisers don't understand how tax can be minimized for owner-managers and professionals.
- Insurance is not usually a good investment vehicle.
- Most owner-managers' investment portfolios take too much risk.

- You can reduce your risk and still retire on your timetable.
- You're probably paying too much in commissions on your investment portfolio.
- Succession planning is not about a transaction that happens when you retire, but a process that should start sooner rather than later.
- The traditional method of extracting income from your business is less tax-effective and less flexible than the dividend method.
- There are some very specific moves you should make to ensure that an untimely death doesn't lead to financial disaster for your family or the loss of your business.
- Despite how complex all of these issues are, there are some very straightforward steps you can take to simplify your life, answer your key questions, eliminate your financial stress, and solve your problems.

Some of these points may be surprising to you. And many of them won't be popular with a lot of people in the financial industry. But it's important for owner-managers and professionals to understand them.

And despite how daunting all of this may sound, there is a very simple, straightforward way to resolve all of your nagging questions, build a plan that's right for you, and set you and your family on the right track. We call that approach *The Golden Telescope*. And here's the good news: going through this process doesn't necessarily mean you have to be put on a financial "diet" and cut back on your spending. Many of the clients we work with end up having more cash to spend after they go through this process, because they had been paying too much in fees and/or taxes.

Why do we call this plan a "telescope"? First, because accountants and financial planners like us, who work specifically with clients like you, focus on the long-term. We try to look far into the future — maybe not light years ahead, but certainly decades. And second, because a telescope needs to be properly supported and balanced — otherwise, you won't see anything meaningful. As Sandra is about to discover when she goes shopping for Katie, the tripod is just as important as the telescope. You can't get a clear picture of the horizon with just one or two legs; you need all three to work in balance. And in financial planning, the three legs that must be integrated are *tax and accounting, financial planning and investment management.*

Based on viewing that long-term horizon with focus and balance, *The Golden Telescope* consists of six simple rules for addressing your unique needs:

1. **Beware insurance pitfalls and traps.** We'll show you why you likely have too much or the wrong life insurance. You may be surprised when you find out what you really need.
2. **Slash your taxes.** We'll show you how you can capitalize on your position as an owner-manager or professional to keep a lot more of your own money and give less of it away unnecessarily to the government. You'll end up with more cash to spend on the things you want now and in the future.
3. **Reduce your risk without changing your timetable.** Your investment portfolio is probably too aggressive. We'll show you an approach with less risk that doesn't mean you have to change your timetable for retirement.
4. **Throw out the cookie-cutter.** You can't have the same financial plan as someone with entirely different circumstances. We'll show you how to get a real financial plan and make sure it covers everything and everyone in your life.
5. **Talk to your family. Now.** Succession planning is an uncomfortable topic for many people because it's complicated and tricky. But we'll show you how to replace anxiety and uncertainty with clarity and peace of mind by starting the process at the right time and approaching it in a way that dramatically reduces the inevitable family tensions.
6. **Hire a quarterback.** Your clients or patients choose you because you're the best at what you do. You should do the same: recruit a trusted, expert adviser who can look after your financial requirements with a full understanding of your needs while you focus on work and family.

In the pages ahead, we'll explain each of these six rules in detail, and illustrate them by using more of the storyline of Gary and Jennifer and Sandra and Mike. The characters aren't real, but they and their situations are very realistic, based on thousands of interactions we've had with clients just like you. We hope you'll find this makes what we have to say not only a little bit more entertaining than a typical financial textbook, but also a powerful illustration of the lessons and principles.

By following the six simple rules of *The Golden Telescope*, you can organize your affairs in a few steps, and then go back to doing what you do best: building your business or your practice. Only from now on, you'll have the peace of mind of knowing that the value you're creating will be protected from unnecessary risk and structured in the way that will create the highest benefit for you and the people you love. And that you'll be ready for many of the challenges that may present themselves in the years ahead.

We want to stress once again that the principles of *The Golden Telescope* apply specifically to people like you. Despite the abundance of personal financial books on the market, there's very little tailored to owner-managers and professionals. That's what many people in the financial industry simply don't understand: your needs are different from those of your friends with different careers.

*The Golden Telescope* will help you find the answers to the questions you have about your future and help you avoid all the pitfalls of your circumstances. You'll be able to navigate through seemingly complex decisions and considerations, like how to transfer wealth to your family in the most effective manner, how to choose the right investment strategy, how to handle succession planning, what insurance is right for you, and what is absolutely wrong.

STEP ONE

# 1 BEWARE
## INSURANCE
## PITFALLS
## AND TRAPS

As Gary finished his drink, Mike looked up and saw another club member approaching the table.

"Here we go," he said.

"What?" asked Gary.

"It's Ron Anderson. The insurance guy."

"No, it's okay. I've been talking to him." Gary turned around. "Ron, pull up a chair."

Ron sat down. He had a big smile on his face. "Hi guys," he said. "Can I get you another round?"

"I'm okay," said Mike. "I have to go anyway."

"Stick around, I won't interrupt for long," said Ron. "How was your game?"

"Don't ask," said Gary.

"I've got a bit of a streak going," said Mike.

"Well done, Mike," said Ron. He turned to Gary. "I've got those numbers we talked about," he said, and pulled a folder out of his bag. "I figured I might run into you," Ron continued. "We don't have to talk about this now. But I thought I'd give you this package and you could look at it when you have a minute."

"Are you sure you don't want me to —" asked Mike.

"No, it's fine," said Gary.

Mike pulled out his phone in order to appear to be doing something else. He saw an email from Sandra with a question about telescopes.

Gary flipped through the proposal quickly. He was the kind of guy who liked to go to the last page right away rather than read through the whole sales pitch. At his dealership, the prices were right on the cars, not buried in some eight-page document. Why couldn't everyone operate like that?

"So I'd be putting a hundred grand a year into this?"

"Yes, but if you read through the presentation, you'll see it's not just insurance," said Ron. "It's an investment. It's not unusual for someone of your income and net worth to use this kind of instrument."

"Still, it seems like a lot of money," said Gary. He winked at Mike. "That's like, you know, two or three per cent of my annual income."

Mike chuckled. "Or one month of losses on the stock market," he said.

"If you do things the right way, as I've spelled them out here, there are tax advantages to putting your money in insurance," said Ron.

"But can I get the money back out if I need it?" asked Gary.

"You can always borrow against your policy if you need to. It's an asset that's building in value. There are some charts and graphs in there that show how much it would be worth over time."

"Okay, leave it with me," said Gary.

"No problem," said Ron. "But don't leave it too long. You don't want something to happen to you in the meantime that could prevent you from getting coverage. If you want, I can pop by your office next week and we can talk more."

He turned to Mike. "Let me know if you and your wife ever need any help with your finances," he said. "I'd be happy to take a look at things and make some recommendations."

"Okay," said Mike, trying to sound polite but not too encouraging. "I will."

"Cheers, guys!" said Ron as he stood up from the table. "I'll call you to set up an appointment, Gary."

Mike watched Ron walk out the door of the clubhouse. "Well, that was interesting," he said. "If I wrote up a proposal asking you to give me $100,000 a year, would you take a look at it?"

"Well, it's not going to him, is it?" said Gary. "It's an investment."

"Are you sure it's what you need?"

Gary looked down again at the insurance folder. One more decision to make. Now Ron had him thinking about the prospect of getting sick and what that might mean for his family. On top of that, he had to figure out how to tell Jennifer about his miserable stock portfolio, satisfy her appeals to spend more time in Florida, and respond to his kids' requests to have more input into the business: It was all adding up. Not to mention that putt he missed on the 18th green.

Gary looked up at Mike.

"I know as much about this stuff as you do about astronomy," he said.

Gary is a high-profile local business owner with a high net worth and a solid income, so it's inevitable that someone has approached him about insurance. And since he's struggled with managing his finances on his own, it's only natural that he would consider getting some help from someone like Ron, a fellow member at his golf club.

So what should Gary do?

Life insurance is a useful tool, especially for a business owner like Gary. But we often see business owners and professionals with the wrong insurance for their needs.

Here's a good example of why that happens. Not long ago, a client came to us with a financial plan prepared by an insurance broker. Even if you're not a financial expert, if you looked at this plan you'd probably be able to tell pretty quickly that it isn't a plan at all, but instead a carefully constructed rationale for buying the very products that the broker was selling. Just because you write "financial plan" on the cover page doesn't make it a real financial plan. Based on the many examples of this that we've seen over the years, we give the following advice to all our clients:

**AVOID INSURANCE AS AN INVESTMENT, ESPECIALLY WHEN YOU'RE PROMISED HIGH RETURNS AND TAX SAVINGS.**

That's a strong statement. But based on what we've witnessed over more than 30 years of working with clients like Gary, it's true. And since insurance is often costly and requires a long-term commitment, the mistakes that some clients make can have huge consequences for them and their families.

Here's a simple fact: most of the people selling insurance don't understand the unique requirements of business owners and professionals and their complicated tax situations.

Here's what the insurance industry often tells people like Gary:

- "Insurance is always a great investment." That's wrong.
- "It's a great tax savings vehicle no matter what your situation." Also wrong.
- "You can always borrow against your policy." Wrong again.

In Gary's case, the proposal to put $100,000 per year in a universal life policy is not based on any assessment of his situation. Here's why we'd advise against it:

- Gary doesn't have the cash flow to pay the annual premium. Despite his significant income and net worth, Gary doesn't have enough money left over after he pays the bills to put $100,000 into insurance.
- The products recommended by his pal at the golf club have management fees that are a lot higher than Gary's other investment options.
- The financial plan has some pretty aggressive assumptions regarding what Gary will earn through the investments in his insurance portfolio. If those aren't realistic, Gary could end up with a lot less money than his friend is forecasting.
- The investments also don't take into account the rest of Gary's portfolio. Do they balance well with the rest of his holdings? Do they reflect his risk profile as a business owner? No.
- A universal life policy is likely not what Gary needs at this stage of his career.

Before investing in insurance, especially to the tune of $100,000 a year, you need to take a step back and evaluate your entire financial picture. Gary's situation may not be the same as yours, but there are many things to consider as you evaluate insurance and investment options, including:

- How large is your net worth?
- How much of your wealth is tied up in your business?
- Have you paid off all of your debt, or are you still carrying a mortgage?
- Have you used all of the room in your RRSPs and TFSAs?
- Do you have a partner who is going to take over your business when you die, or will it go to your spouse or children?
- Is the value of your business dependent on your day-to-day involvement? Is there a risk that you'll lose substantial value and your business will be sold in a fire sale on your death?

Buying insurance is a tricky business. So once you've answered those questions about your financial situation, you also need to make sure you avoid a number of pitfalls that can lead an owner or professional to make the wrong decisions:

- There's a lack of transparency about commissions in life insurance. Many policies have commissions that are front-end loaded, meaning an insurance agent may be selling a policy to you because it's in his best interests, not yours. Just try asking what the commission is and see what response you get.
- Some universal policies also have fees and taxes that come right off your investment at the front end. You think you're putting in a certain amount of money, but you've actually lost a huge chunk of your "investment" right up front.
- You can gauge an insurance or investment product's fees and commissions by determining how much you would get back if you collapsed the policy within a year or two.
- If you are a new professional, don't get trapped into buying a

universal life or whole life policy. Your life insurance needs in the early stage of your career can be covered by a less expensive group insurance plan through your professional association, or a personal term policy.

- Universal life or whole life policies can be useful for estate planning, but usually only after you've accumulated a lot of wealth and have no debt. They are not a good investment vehicle for younger professionals or owners.
- Segregated funds are often promoted as a good tool for business owners and professionals because they offer protection against creditors. But the vast majority of clients like you don't actually need creditor proofing, so they should stay away from segregated funds because they are extremely expensive products.

Having said all of this, we must stress: We believe in insurance. It's important to have the right amount of insurance for the right reasons. But you can waste a lot of money on the wrong insurance that doesn't accomplish what you need for your specific circumstances.

Here's what we've done with clients like Gary. First of all, Gary was approached by someone who was trying to sell him insurance as an investment vehicle. We don't think that's a good solution to his needs, especially since he doesn't have the cash flow to fund the premiums his pal is recommending. So we're going to split the two issues and talk about what we recommend for his insurance requirements. We'll talk more about his investment objectives later.

Just because Gary doesn't need insurance as an investment doesn't mean that he doesn't need insurance. Let's review his situation. Unlike other business owners, Gary has his kids working in the business, meaning the company would not need to be sold if Gary weren't around anymore. So there isn't the risk of a huge taxable capital gain if Gary died suddenly, as his shares would be transferred to Jennifer on a tax-deferred basis and the kids would assume management responsibilities.

And Gary doesn't need to use an insurance policy as a savings vehicle. Besides, he doesn't have the cash flow for the $100,000 a year in premiums.

Gary might benefit from a term policy that would cover some short-term expenses that Jennifer might need to cover if he were to die before she did. That, however, would probably be a policy with a benefit of a few hundred thousand dollars, not millions. In terms of a larger policy, if Gary's kids weren't ready to take over the business, we'd investigate a simple term policy with a sufficient benefit to pay the capital gains tax his family would incur if they sold the business. That's the most cost-effective way to deal with that tax risk.

In Gary's case, however, the most likely scenario is that if he dies, his kids will run the business and his wife will own his shares in the company. So what we need to address is what happens when both Gary and Jennifer are gone. A joint-and-last-to-die policy covering both spouses would cover the capital gains tax when the second spouse dies.

Gary is just one example, of course, and what's right for him isn't necessarily the best option for you. But the point is that insurance salesmen like Ron aren't trained or compensated to offer the best solution for Gary or you. Beware the advice you get from insurance reps, and get some impartial help to figure out what's best for your unique circumstances. Otherwise, like Gary, you could be putting thousands of dollars every month into something you don't need.

## SUMMARY

Here are the key points you should remember about insurance:

- There are a lot of pitfalls that lead owners and professionals to choose the wrong insurance.
- Be wary of insurance brokers who don't understand your unique circumstances as a business owner or professional and who promote the benefits of insurance as an investment, as collateral, or as a tax-savings vehicle.

- You should almost never buy insurance primarily as an investment or income-sheltering solution. Instead, it's the most cost-effective tool to deal with unique business issues like capital gains, paying off creditors, buy-sell agreements for business partners, and equalizing inheritance among family members.
- There are circumstances in which it may be appropriate for you to invest in a permanent insurance policy like a universal life policy, but only if it's part of an integrated solution that takes into consideration your tax situation and estate plan.
- Before you choose the right insurance, you need to have a complete picture of your goals and your financial situation.

STEP TWO

# 2 SLASH
Y O U R
**TAXES**

As the kids scampered away from the table to return to their movie, Mike gathered up the plates and walked over to the sink. He dumped the remaining few scraps into the garbage and took a small amount of pride in the fact that his two children finished almost all the food he had prepared. It wasn't always so easy.

He heard the door open in the front hall.

"Hi there," he said. Sandra walked into the kitchen, threw her keys on the table, slung her bag over a chair and exhaled loudly.

"Long day?" he asked.

"If this were a 1950s TV show, I'd be pouring myself a drink right now."

"If this were a 1950s TV show, you'd be pouring me a drink right now," said Mike.

Sandra smiled. "Aw, wouldn't it be nice to come home to supper on the table, the smell of bread baking in the oven?" she teased him.

"You tell me," said Mike. "I didn't bake any bread, but I made you some chicken and asparagus."

"Thanks," said Sandra.

"Did you get a chance to look for Katie's gift?"

"I browsed a bit online. But do you think it's too serious a gift for a nine-year-old?"

"It's what she keeps asking for," said Mike. "And we had such a hard time getting the telescope to work last night."

"All right, but if we get this, you won't have any more excuses," said Sandra. "So how was your game today?"

"I won," said Mike. "Again. Either I'm getting better or he's getting a lot worse."

Sandra took a plate out of the cupboard and began serving

herself some supper.

"Anyway, Gary and I got talking today," said Mike. "You think we have financial worries. You should hear about the situation he's in."

Mike remembered that Gary had asked him not to tell Sandra. Maybe he should hold off on telling her all the details.

"Is this about him losing a half -a-million dollars on the stock market?"

"What? How do you know about that?"

"Oh, I know all the details."

"From Jennifer? Really? Gary doesn't think she knows."

"Oh, she knows," said Sandra. "She knows plenty."

"I can't believe you found out before me."

"I always find out stuff like that before you. It's because women talk and men golf."

"Well, we talked about a couple of things today," said Mike, seeing an opportunity.

Then he paused. This was a bit of a risky gambit, introducing the cottage discussion at the end of a long day for Sandra. And he realized almost as soon as the words left his mouth that the setup wasn't exactly ideal. For one thing, it was going to sound like he and his buddy had been talking about the merits of buying a cottage, and now he was going to use that conversation to convince his wife. Plus, as Mike had just pointed out, Gary didn't exactly have a lot of credibility about financial issues. And the fact that they were talking about it over a leisurely beer at the golf club wasn't going to help his cause.

But he was already committed.

"Go on," said Sandra.

"Well, I think we should revisit the idea of getting a cottage."

Sandra cut into a piece of chicken. Without looking up, she said, "I thought we decided to wait."

"But why should we wait? If other people can afford it, why can't we? I don't want to wait until the kids are too old to enjoy it."

"What's the point of having a cottage if I'm just going to have to work weekends to pay for it?" said Sandra. "I'll never be there."

"Do you really need to do extra work for us to have a cottage? That doesn't make any sense to me. We've got lots of money coming in."

"We've also got lots of money going out," said Sandra. "We're talking about putting both our kids in private school. That could be $50,000 a year."

"Even so, between the two of us, even with my modest earnings, we should have enough to enjoy life."

"I know what you mean, Mike. But you don't know what it's like carrying the financial burden for all of us. Not just you and the kids, but my parents too. Now that they are here in Canada, I'm responsible for them. And it's not just the burden of earning the money, but also worrying that we're setting aside enough for the future. Nobody else worries about that except me."

"I worry about that too," said Mike.

"But you think it's all going to work out in the end. You don't think about what will happen if something goes wrong."

"If something goes wrong, we can sell the cottage."

"I know you think I'm being way too cautious," said Sandra. "But there are a lot of factors to consider before we make a big decision like that. One of my partners said she and her husband just went through this. She's suggesting I talk to someone at her bank."

"Well, that's okay with me," said Mike. "I'm not in a rush. I just want to make sure we enjoy life."

"I can't enjoy life if I'm stressed out about money," said Sandra.

"Well then maybe you should talk to this bank person."

Just then, Mike and Sandra's son ran in from the family room.

"Mommy, Daddy! There's a whole new Cars area at Disney World. It looks really, really cool. Can we —"

"Not now," said Mike and Sandra together.

To many people, Sandra's concerns are almost incomprehensible. How can she be worried about money? As Mike asks, how can they not afford a cottage?

But Sandra's situation is not unique. She thinks she has a cash-flow problem, that she and Mike don't have enough income to cover their existing expenditures plus new investments like a cottage and private school, while still saving enough for their retirement. We see that kind of anxiety in clients all the time, even with people who make as much as Sandra or more.

But rather than a cash flow problem, it's quite likely that Sandra has a different issue: she's paying too much in fees and taxes. She could be saving just as much money for tomorrow and still be putting more toward today's priorities, as Mike is suggesting. We see this over and over again among high-income professionals and business owners:

## WHAT LOOKS LIKE A CASH-FLOW PROBLEM IS OFTEN AN ISSUE OF TOO MUCH IN FEES AND TAXES.

By this we don't mean that people should stop worrying about cash flow and just start spending more money on cottages and vacations. But by taking a strategic approach to your finances and employing some of the principles we're about to outline, you can reduce taxes and fees and have more money to spend today without compromising your long-term savings.

The first step is one that Sandra has already taken. Professionals like Sandra – physicians, dentists, and others – should set up a private corporation. If you own a business, you probably already have a corporation and perhaps even a holding company, so these benefits apply to you as well. There are significant advantages to incorporation, including:

- If you aren't spending all of your annual income, you can leave some of it in the corporation and defer paying personal income tax on it until you take it out.
- You'll pay corporate tax as you earn the money, but at a much lower rate than personal tax.
- A professional corporation can act as another nest egg in which

you can build retirement savings. But you have much more control over this pot of money and how and when you access it compared to government-regulated instruments like RRSPs.

- Unlike an RRSP, you don't have to start taking money out when you hit a certain age. You don't have to draw the pool down by a certain amount every year.
- If you die with money still left in the company, you can leave the shares – and the same level of control – to your heirs, unlike an RRSP, which is immediately deregistered on the death of the second spouse.
- If you are a physician or a dentist in Ontario, you can use a professional corporation to income split with your spouse. If your wife or husband is earning significantly less than you are, you can take advantage of that lower tax rate.

Sandra recently incorporated on the advice of some of her fellow radiologists. But she isn't taking full advantage of this new situation. Indeed, she's missing out on the biggest opportunity arising from incorporation: the dividend method.

Sandra is under the impression that the best way to disburse the income she needs from her professional corporation is in the form of a salary. She was told by an adviser that unless she pays out her income as salary, she won't have any RRSP room and won't be able to take advantage of the tax savings that result from that. The advice she received: pay yourself at least enough salary to maximize your RRSP contributions.

But here's an important lesson:

**PAYING YOURSELF A SALARY TO MAXIMIZE YOUR RRSP CONTRIBUTIONS IS PROBABLY NOT THE BEST WAY FOR YOU TO RECEIVE YOUR INCOME. IN FACT, THE TRADITIONAL METHOD OF EXTRACTING SALARY FROM YOUR BUSINESS IS LESS TAX-EFFECTIVE AND LESS FLEXIBLE THAN EITHER THE DIVIDEND METHOD OR A COMBINATION OF DIVIDENDS AND SALARY**

Indeed, we recommend to many of our clients that they use dividends to pay out the money inside their corporations. The dividend method has many advantages over salary, so many that they typically outweigh the benefits of creating RRSP room. But if you are concerned about being sued and not having enough insurance, then an RRSP is a more secure location for your investments.

If you are a physician or dentist or a business owner, in most places in Canada you can set up any adult member of your family as a shareholder in your company, allowing them to earn dividends on very favourable terms. If you are a member of a different profession, you may be able to use a related company for income-splitting. Shareholders without other income can be paid a $40,000 to $50,000 dividend without any additional income tax beyond the corporate income tax already paid by the company.

So in Sandra's case, if she makes her parents shareholders in her professional corporation, she can pay each of them $40,000 to $50,000 per year. And neither she nor they will incur any additional income tax consequences. That's a much less expensive way of getting money to them.

And when her kids turn 18, she can make them shareholders and pay each of them $40,000 to $50,000 a year tax-free for their university and other expenses. If they do attend university, she could pay them an additional amount in dividends equal to the amount of their education tax credits.

The dividend method can give Sandra a lot of options and boost her cash flow. She should still pay herself a salary of at least $6,000 per year to qualify for the employment tax credit on her personal tax return, and to be eligible for disability benefits under CPP. If she had childcare expenses to deduct, then a higher salary would make sense. But otherwise, she can pay herself and her family members dividends to extract money from her corporation in the most tax-effective way possible.

And that's just one of the benefits of incorporating, and only one of the ways you can reduce what you pay in taxes. By using a corporation properly and effectively, you will have many tools at your disposal, including income splitting with your spouse. Depending on your circumstances, there may be advantages to deferring taxes and investing money within your corporation. Sandra and Mike could probably afford to buy a cottage. At the very least, she could stop worrying so much about money.

## SUMMARY

Here are the key points you should remember about managing your income:

- There are significant advantages to incorporation if you are a professional.
- Whether you're a physician or a dentist in Ontario or a business owner, you should use income splitting to take advantage of lower tax rates paid by other members of your family. Other professionals may be able to use a related company for income-splitting.
- If you have extra money, you can leave it in your corporation to defer taxes.
- Your corporation can be a much more effective nest egg than RRSPs, especially since you are not required by law to take money out at a certain age and at specific intervals.
- The traditional salary-only method of extracting income from your business is less tax-effective and less flexible than the dividend method or a combination of the two.
- Using a corporation to its full advantage, including engaging in income splitting and having family members as shareholders, can dramatically reduce your taxes and improve your cash flow.
- You can pay a dividend of up to $40,000 to $50,000 to a parent or adult child without any additional income tax consequences beyond the tax already paid by the company if they don't have other sources of income.

You should still pay yourself a salary of at least $6,000 per year to qualify for the employment tax credit on your personal tax return, and to be eligible for disability benefits under CPP.

STEP THREE

# 3 REDUCE

## YOUR RISK

WITHOUT CHANGING
YOUR TIMETABLE

As Gary walked back to his office in the far corner of the showroom, his mood was brighter than when he had left the golf course the afternoon before.

His talk with Mike had left him a bit discouraged. It was nothing Mike had said or done, although that last missed putt was still on his mind. But by talking through his finances with Mike, Gary suddenly felt like there were a lot of missed putts in the rest of his life, a lot of things he should have gotten to by now but had never had the time for.

He had always assumed that by this point in his life, things would have started to get a bit easier. After more than 20 years of owning his own dealership, he had expected to have enough money to retire, whether he chose to do so or not. He had expected that by now he would have groomed one of his kids to take over.

But Gary realized on his way home from the golf course that he had never planned for any of these things. He had always thought he could do that later. Or, more accurately, he thought many of those things would take care of themselves. He knew now that he should have gotten on top of a lot of that stuff a lot sooner. But there was always a reason why he hadn't, like the fact that he was busy building and expanding his business.

Today, though, Gary felt a bit better. He was back in his element, talking to customers, managing his employees, and solving problems. The dealership was having a good morning and a good week. Sales were up over last year, and Gary was enjoying doing what he did best: working on deals that were good for his customers and good for his dealership.

Maybe Jennifer was right. He needed to let go a bit and start spending more time away from the office, maybe stay another week or two at their place in Florida. He would tell her that tonight.

Gary sat down at his desk. Along with the latest reports from his sales manager was the folder that Ron the insurance agent had given him the day before. He wasn't sure about putting that much money into insurance. On the other hand, what he'd been doing so far wasn't working.

As he did whenever he had a spare moment, about 10 or 12 times a day, Gary logged into his stock tracking website to see how his portfolio was performing. While he'd lost a lot in the last 18 months, the past week had been fairly good. Yesterday had been one of the best days in the last six months.

But today the markets were dropping. Gary's portfolio was down again. He turned on the TV in his office, which was always set to the business news channel. Most of the scrolling numbers at the bottom of the screen had red arrows next to them, pointing downward. The anchor had a very concerned look on his face.

Gary picked up the newspaper and pulled out the business section. He found his favourite column, the one that recommended stocks to buy and avoid. Nothing in his portfolio was listed as being a "dud," so that was good news. Gary jotted down a few of the recommended picks, the "stars," on his notepad. Then he started reading an article about a new investment strategy. It was accompanied by a colourful pie chart that showed a detailed breakdown of the mix of individual stocks, funds, bonds, and other instruments that was considered, at least by the writer, to be the ideal combination to achieve maximum returns.

Gary looked up briefly from the article, and something caught his attention. Jennifer was walking into the dealership. Through the glass wall of his office, he could see her opening the front door and smiling at Robin, the receptionist, as she turned toward his corner of the building.

It was unusual for Jennifer to show up at the office unannounced. Was something wrong with one of the kids? No, she would have called his cell phone, as she had when Carter broke his wrist playing soccer. Had Gary forgotten that it was their anniversary? No, that was in August. Was he supposed to have met her somewhere, or picked her up, or swapped cars with her, or something like that?

He racked his mind for an explanation. Nothing came to him before Jennifer walked in the room, shut the door, put her purse on his desk, and sat down in the chair across from him.

"Hi honey," she said.

"Hi babe," said Gary. "What are you doing here?"

"I have an appointment with you," said Jennifer.

"What?" Gary looked at the calendar on his computer. Sure enough, there was an hour blocked off for "Jennifer." But he hadn't put it there.

"I asked Robin to schedule me in," said Jennifer.

"Are you going to buy a car?" Gary joked nervously. He wasn't used to being caught off guard at the dealership, being at a disadvantage to the person sitting across from him in his own office.

"I think we should talk to a financial adviser," said Jennifer. "Together."

Until now, of course, Gary had always looked after managing the family's money. Jennifer, he always joked, looked after spending it.

"Jennifer," he said. "Don't worry about that stuff. It's all taken care of."

"Is it?" she asked. She pulled a piece of paper out of her purse. "Because based on this, I don't think it is."

Gary's heart rate suddenly increased. Jennifer was unfolding something that looked a lot like a monthly statement from his online brokerage. And that, of course, was exactly what it was. He was suddenly reminded of the time his mother had found his Grade 8 report card in his school bag, the one he hadn't intended to show her.

"What's going on, Gary?" Jennifer asked calmly. "What happened to all our money?"

Gary's mouth was dry, but he began to offer explanations like, "I just got a bit unlucky" and "it's not as bad as it looks."

"Why are you managing our portfolio anyway?" Jennifer asked. "Don't you have a business to run?"

Gary shifted some papers on his desk so that the article about the new investment strategy was now covered by some car brochures.

"I followed a lot of good advice that I had read," Gary said. "My portfolio was really diversified, just like they said it should be."

"Who is 'they'?" asked Jennifer. "I don't want to rely on advice from people on TV or in the newspaper. We need to talk to someone who understands our situation and has more experience with this stuff than we do." She wasn't as angry as Gary had expected her to be.

"I just want to make sure we're on the right track," she continued. "I also think it's time to start planning who's going to take over the business. It doesn't mean it has to happen right away. But we can start talking about it."

"By the way," said Gary. "I think you're right. We should spend more time at our place in Florida."

"I'm glad to hear that," said Jennifer. "But don't change the subject."

It's natural for successful people like Gary to expect big returns from their investments. They`re used to winning and don't want to settle for being average. But it isn't wise to plan for high returns, because they carry much higher risk. And here's the critical thing: those higher returns often aren't necessary.

This is one of the most significant things we tell our clients:

**YOU MAY NOT NEED A HUGE RATE OF RETURN TO ACHIEVE YOUR INVESTMENT GOALS. MANY BUSINESS OWNERS AND PROFESSIONALS CAN ACCOMPLISH THEIR OBJECTIVES WITH MUCH LESS RISK AND VOLATILITY.**

This is something that surprises a lot of people, but it becomes evident when you prepare a proper financial plan. You might be taking on more risk than you need to in order to achieve your goals. The returns you're striving for might be more than you need. And that level of risk might hurt your chances of meeting your goals and cause you a lot of stress and anxiety in the meantime.

In Gary's case, he went after aggressive results that were surplus to his requirements. He did that partly because he's a competitive guy who doesn't like the idea that other people might be earning a bigger return than he does. But his aggressive approach also came about because he hasn't taken a comprehensive look at his entire situation. He doesn't realize that he has enough on his balance sheet that he doesn't need to get big returns in order to have enough money to retire. In the end, he got burned by his aggressive strategy.

But there's another reason why Gary should be following a much more conservative investment strategy.

As a business owner, there's already some risk in Gary's life. His business is doing well now, but that might not always be the case. Gary makes a lot of money, but there's less long-term security to his job than if he were a high-school teacher with a guaranteed pension. If the car company affiliated with his dealership has a bad year, so does Gary.

So Gary shouldn't be compounding his risk with an aggressive investment strategy. If anything, he needs a safer approach to his investments than someone who doesn't own a business.

If you're going to follow a less-aggressive and less-risky investment strategy and still achieve your long-term financial objectives, there are three key steps you can take to maximize your returns:

1. Chose an adviser whose fee structure is aligned with your goals.
2. If you have sufficient funds, use a discretionary money manager with low management fees to increase your chances of success.
3. Rely on a custom plan for asset mix and location, and rebalance regularly.

Gary shouldn't be looking after his own portfolio any more than his customers should be looking after their own brakes. He has a business to run. Our first piece of advice to clients is always, "Don't try to do it all yourself."

If you've been looking after your own portfolio and you've been successful, count yourself lucky. It's not as easy as you made it look. And just because you've done well so far doesn't mean you always will.

But don't choose just any adviser. Our advice is to stay away from anyone who promises to beat the market by a big margin. Nobody can predict the future, not even the advisers who did well last year.

The odds are that they were just lucky. There's a lot of evidence that shows that advisers who do really well one year are no more likely to be successful the following year than any of their competitors.

**IF AN INVESTMENT ADVISER PROMISES TO BEAT THE MARKET BY A SIGNIFICANT MARGIN, RUN IN THE OTHER DIRECTION.**

**AND THE EASIEST WAY TO INCREASE YOUR RETURN IS TO REDUCE YOUR INVESTMENT FEES AND TAXES.**

Here's another important consideration when you are choosing an adviser, one that is almost always overlooked: Don't go with anyone whose fee structure is not aligned with your goals. Many financial advisers get paid based on activity, earning commissions whenever you make a trade, regardless of how it works out. So guess what? They keep recommending trades and other transactions.

Even more concerning is the fact that some fees are often not transparent to you as the client. It's your money that's being moved around, but do you know for sure how much commission your adviser is making? If a particular fund pays a higher commission, can you be sure your adviser is choosing it because it's best for your needs?

We strongly recommend choosing an adviser who charges a transparent fee based on assets under administration, who manages rather than sells, and who benefits when you benefit. With this approach, you pay a fee every year based on the total size of your portfolio, regardless of which investments they choose. So their interests are aligned with yours instead of possibly being at cross purposes.

To some people, this type of fee looks like an additional cost. But it's not. Advisers will tell you commissions are paid by the mutual funds, but of course the mutual funds get the money to pay those commissions from your investment. So either way, you are paying. You're better off knowing what your cost is and having that alignment of interests with your adviser. And here's another advantage: if it's outside your registered investments like RRSPs, the management fee is tax deductible.

Speaking of fees, every mutual fund has a management fee built into it. This is the cost of administering the fund itself. And those fees have a big impact on your return. Look at it this way: a fund that charges a two per cent fee has to grow by two per cent just to maintain your initial investment. So if you invest in a fund with a lower fee, your chances of your portfolio growing are higher. This is especially true in an environment with low interest rates and low returns.

There are good funds that charge low management fees but still produce returns comparable to other funds with higher fees. Make sure you understand all the fees you're being charged.

Another critical component to generating good returns without high risk is asset allocation. There's an increasing body of research that shows asset allocation has a huge impact on results; it can represent more than 90 per cent of the equation. Having the right asset mix is much more important and effective than choosing individual stocks or funds.

Gary told Jennifer he had a diversified portfolio. But most people think they are more diversified than they really are. They might choose a wide selection of mutual funds and think that achieves diversity. But those funds might all be heavily invested in one group of companies, like the major banks.

So the right asset mix is crucial. But it's also critical to recalibrate that asset allocation as different parts of your portfolio grow at different rates. If 10 per cent of your portfolio is in a particular asset class that grows more rapidly than others, it could soon represent 15 per cent or more of the mix. You need to rebalance the mix regularly; otherwise, it won't be properly diversified anymore.

Some people, like Gary, don't like the idea of buying and holding. They're too impatient to see immediate results, and they react to the latest trends they hear in the financial press. But buying and holding works, as long as you rebalance the asset mix on a regular basis. And something that many financial advisers do not realize is that *where* you hold specific types of assets can be just as important as the mix itself. Research shows that this is one of the most critical factors in the after-tax return you generate with your investments: minimizing your tax bill by putting the right investments in the right places, or what we call asset location.

As just one example, if you have a mix of equities and interest-bearing investments in your portfolio, some advisers will have you hold the same mix in every place you are holding assets (RRSPs, TFSAs, your corporation). But it can be better to have all the equities held in your corporation or a non-registered plan and all the interest-bearing investments in your RRSP, for tax reasons. So it's not just having the right mix, but where you put the different pieces that make up the mix. With expertise in tax policy, an accountant would understand this in a way that many financial advisers wouldn't.

There is so much more to investing, especially as it fits into an overall financial plan, like the one we'll describe in the next chapter.

Our last piece of advice is not to micromanage your investments. If you have a solid plan, you don't need to look at your results more than quarterly. Don't get caught up in the hype of watching market coverage on a daily basis and tracking your investments like the results of your favourite hockey team. That will only cause you unnecessary stress and anxiety.

Investing is like carrying a cup of coffee that's been filled to the brim. If you look at it too closely you're more likely to react, overcompensate and spill. Look straight ahead, and walk steadily and confidently.

## SUMMARY

Here are the key points you should remember about investing:

- If you're an entrepreneur or business owner, you should take into account the risk associated with your business income. A business owner's investment strategy might need to be more conservative than that of a public servant with a guaranteed pension.
- The best advisers start with a plan that looks at your needs and

your objectives and calibrates the strategy according to a careful understanding of your situation before considering any investment or insurance products.

- The purpose of an investment strategy is to fund your goals and requirements. If your goal is to hit a jackpot or outperform your friends, you could end up losing big.
- Don't think you can beat the market. It's mathematically impossible for everyone to achieve above-average returns.
- Your investment strategy for your RRSPs shouldn't be in isolation from everything else. It has to be part of a broader plan.
- Beware the risk of being fooled by the aura of past returns. Funds or advisers with a strong track record are lucky, not good. Research shows most of them don't do any better than average the next year.
- Leave your ego out of the equation. Don't overestimate your ability to manage your own money. You're not watching the market full-time. Why would you expect to outperform an industry of people who are?
- Beware investment advisers whose sources of income don't align with your objectives. Instead of transaction-based commissions, front-end loads or deferred sales charges, go with a transparent fee based on assets under administration.
- The right asset mix and asset location are critical factors in your after-tax return.
- Focus on long-term performance; stay disciplined and be patient. Don't track your investments more often than every quarter.
- If you need some money to play with in the market, then decide on how much that is in advance, and make sure it is never more than you would be comfortable losing.
- Your investment strategy should integrate your unique tax situation, and make the most of tax-reducing tactics available in corporations and registered plans.

**4**

STEP FOUR
# THROW OUT
— THE —
# COOKIE
# CUTTER

Sandra and Mike were ushered into the small modular office within their local bank branch. As they sat down, Sandra noticed the posters all around them, featuring a series of happy couples who looked like they were thoroughly enjoying their lives, without a care in the world. There was a younger couple standing in the front hall of what was obviously their brand-new home. There were moving boxes in the corner (which looked pristine and perfectly stacked), and the wife was a few months pregnant, of course. They looked like all their dreams had just come true, and there was nothing left in the world that could cause them any concern.

*Fast-forward six months*, thought Sandra. *Half those boxes still won't be unpacked. The beautiful granite countertop will have a stack of unwashed dishes on it, and those hardwood floors won't have been swept in a week. And you'll be up with your kid at three in the morning, wondering if you'll ever sleep again. Then see how relaxed and cheerful you feel.*

Another poster featured a couple that Sandra figured was carefully chosen to look like they were just old enough to be retired but still young enough to be attractive and fit. The woman's hair was an unnatural colour, halfway between blonde and silver. They were petting a dog on a beach, with big grins on their faces.

The bank's slogan made it all sound very easy. But how was it possible, Sandra wondered, to be that carefree? Surely this couple had children. At their stage of life, of course, their kids would not be as young as Sandra's. Maybe they had one who was just starting a career, and another still in university. Even so, surely they'd still be worried about them: Had the older one chosen the right path? Was she going to settle down with her boyfriend, or was he taking her for granted? Was the younger one studying enough, or was he too busy partying with his friends? Would his liberal arts program lead to any meaningful employment?

These were the concerns Sandra pictured herself having when her kids were older. The future she imagined wasn't one without worries, just different worries from the ones she had today. But they would always be about her family. After all, she and Mike rarely talked about anything other than Katie and Jake. Even when they went away for a weekend in Las Vegas and left the children with Mike's parents, most of their conversations involved speculating about what the two kids were up to without them, fondly remembering moments from their younger days, or planning their futures, maintaining the pretense that, as parents, they had some control over what would happen to their kids when they grew up.

In 20 years, she might be less involved in her kids' day-to-day lives, Sandra thought, but she would never be completely free of thinking about them. There might be a dog and a beach in her future, but the look on her face would be more of mild concern, rather than the joy exhibited by the fake retired couple.

A woman walked into the room. "Hello, Mr. And Mrs. de Sousa," she said.

"Redmond," said Mike. "I'm Mike Redmond."

"And it's Dr. de Sousa," said Sandra. "But you can call me Sandra."

"Sorry about that," said the financial adviser. "I'm Delores. How can I help you today?"

"We don't know a lot about this stuff," said Sandra. "But we think we need a financial plan of some kind."

"I can certainly help you with that," said Delores. She clicked her mouse a couple of times. "Let me just ask you a few questions."

Fifteen minutes later, Delores was printing out a document. She had asked Sandra and Mike a series of questions: How much did they earn, what were their assets and liabilities, when did they want to retire, what were their other long-term goals?

Mike thought the questions sounded pretty standard, but he

wasn't overly concerned. He figured that any impartial assessment of their situation would probably bolster his case. The math simply had to work in his favour. Sandra made a lot of money, so there was no reason for them to scrimp and save. If other people with less income didn't have to count their pennies, why did they? Surely a financial expert would back him up on this, although he was beginning to wonder about the extent to which Delores could be considered an expert.

Sandra was a bit less enthusiastic. She had expected a more comprehensive review of their situation. There were so many things running through her mind, none of which had been covered by the bank employee. What about supporting her parents? What about private school for their kids? What if something went wrong? What sort of insurance did they need? Delores had asked only a couple of questions about their risk tolerance, and she had seemed to point them to a specific answer in both cases, as though she had predetermined their answers just by looking at them.

While Delores stood by the printer, Mike thought back to a previous meeting about their financial goals. About two years earlier, before they were talking about buying a cottage, he and Sandra had gone to see an adviser with a large investment firm. The adviser had spent a fair amount of time with them, and had even produced what he called a custom financial plan.

But in the end, his recommendations seemed to point irrevocably in a very specific direction: the solution to all their problems was to invest a significant amount of money with funds administered by the adviser's firm.

And when Mike had taken the plan home, he noticed a couple of flaws in its assumptions. Mike's parents had given them a gift of $50,000 that year to help with the down payment on their new house. The adviser had added that to Mike's salary, and had projected that as his annual income every year from now until retirement. No wonder he predicted they could retire comfortably when they were in their mid-50s. There was an extra million dollars in income in the plan.

Mike had been hopeful that the adviser's plan would lay out a reasonable savings plan that would allow him and Sandra to worry less about their retirement and spend a bit more money on enjoying life in the meantime. But even he had to admit that the expectations were too aggressive. Mike wasn't an expert, but he could tell that the plan was counting on a rate of return that was too high. And the management fees that went to the investment firm were 2.5 per cent, which seemed like a lot.

In the end, it had just been a frustrating waste of time. The plan sat on the dining room table for a couple of weeks before Mike threw it in the recycling bin. And Sandra went back to worrying as much as she had before. And based on that experience, he didn't blame her.

Delores turned around with a sheaf of papers in her hand. She sorted them quickly into three piles and stapled them together, giving Mike and Sandra each one copy of the document. The package was labelled, "Family Financial Plan."

Sandra and Mike listened carefully as Delores walked them through some of the assumptions and recommendations. But Mike could tell that Sandra was already feeling concerned. The whole process was too superficial.

Sandra glanced over at the wall again. Surely a quarter of an hour was not long enough for her to make the transition from worrying about money to looking like one of those carefree people in the posters.

Over the course of the last 25 years, we've witnessed dozens of what we can only describe as financial plan horror stories. Here are just a few examples:

- One client inherited some money from a relative and went to see a financial adviser. The result was a plan that projected he could retire in four years. How was that possible? The adviser treated his inheritance like part of his annual income and assumed he would bring in the same amount every year. The client was very frustrated at having wasted his time on the process.

- Another client received a financial plan from a major bank that used the wrong tax rate for the income earned in his corporation. As a result, he proposed an aggressive, risky investment strategy to achieve the client's goal of retiring on schedule. The forecast returns were completely unrealistic. We completed a comprehensive plan for the client with the right tax rate, and he was able to follow a much less-risky investment strategy.

- A third client was presented with a plan from a mutual fund company several years ago. The plan assumed an annual return of nine per cent after management fees. Within a few years, the rate of return was down significantly, and the adviser didn't adjust the plan. The client was almost in tears because the results were 'way off track. He thought he would have to work an extra decade to make up for it.

Why are there so many bad financial plans? Two reasons. First, most of the people who are advising clients today aren't qualified to compile a proper plan. Second, they are paid to sell specific products, not protect your interests.

When you go to see a doctor or a lawyer, you can count on the fact that, at a minimum, they've met the standard for the industry, or they wouldn't be allowed to practice. When it comes to financial advisers, you can't make that assumption. According to the Financial Planning Standards Council, there are more than 100,000 financial advisers in Canada. And only 17,000 have the designation of Certified Financial Planner (CFP), with another 400 are Registered Financial Planners (RFP).

That means the other 83 per cent aren't certified, and therefore are not subject to a code of practice standards. And while there is some general regulatory oversight of the industry, it's not as comprehensive as you might think. For example, there are securities regulators. But they regulate transactions, not the financial planning advice that leads to those transactions. A lot of people assume that financial advisers have a legal fiduciary responsibility to work in the best interests of the client, but that is not true.

So when you meet with a financial adviser, is the person sitting across from you a qualified, certified financial planner? Does he or she have your best interests at heart? Does he or she have the knowledge, experience and skills to understand your needs and put them first?

A proper financial plan takes time — a lot longer than the 15 minutes it took the bank representative to spit out a template for Sandra and Mike. In the meeting with Delores, Sandra raised a lot of questions. The plan should answer those questions.

In fact, here's what a proper financial plan should include:

- Goals and objectives
- Personal and corporate net worth assessments
- Cash-flow planning, both corporate and personal
- Tax planning
- Retirement planning
- Investment management
- Estate planning
- Risk management (insurance)

The point is not that you need a whole bunch of documents, but that without them you'll get bad advice. Would you rather make decisions based on complete or incomplete information? Would you want your doctor to make a diagnosis and recommend treatment based on a superficial assessment or a comprehensive one?

And although it may sound daunting, you don't have to do all the work. A CFP or RFP will ask you a lot of questions and produce something that meets your needs.

Here's why a plan is so important:

**FINANCIAL PLANNING IS MORE THAN JUST INVESTMENT ADVICE. THE PURPOSE OF SEEING A FINANCIAL ADVISER IS NOT TO HELP YOU PICK SPECIFIC PRODUCTS, BUT TO CHOOSE THE RIGHT PATH FOR THE FUTURE. SO THE REAL VALUE OF FINANCIAL ADVICE ISN'T IN PRODUCT RECOMMENDATIONS, BUT IN THE BROADER FINANCIAL PLANNING ADVICE THAT SHOULD BE PROVIDED BEFORE ANY SPECIFIC PRODUCTS ARE EVEN CONTEMPLATED.**

Bigger questions like whether to put money into RRSPs or pay down debt and what asset mix is appropriate are far more important than any specific product recommendations.

But the vast majority of advisers are only compensated if they sell a product. So they aren't interested in the bigger picture. They don't make any money if they tell you to pay down debt, even if that's the best thing for you to do.

And as an owner-manager or professional, you face big questions that most financial advisers can't or won't answer. For example, a lot of financial planners don't have the capacity to deal with corporations and their tax implications. They don't know enough information about them and how they work to give you the best advice. Delores hasn't even asked Sandra about whether or not she has a professional corporation.

Once again, the cookie-cutter doesn't apply to you.

Here's just one example of how good advice and good decisions come out of a complete and comprehensive financial plan: If you have surplus money in a corporation, a financial adviser may recommend investing it to generate a return. But if a proper financial plan is completed, it might be clear that the best option could be to take money out of the company in a tax-favourable way and pay down personal debt.

Another example applies directly to Gary and Jennifer. They

own a property in the US. There are material tax implications to owning foreign property that could come into play when making major financial decisions. If they aren't taken into account in a proper financial plan, the consequences could be huge.

Ultimately, it's impossible to make good decisions if you don't have good, complete information. So without a proper financial plan, you can't have the peace of mind that you're doing the right thing for the right reasons, rather than guessing and waiting to see how things will turn out.


## SUMMARY

Here are the key points you should remember about financial planning:

- There's a big distinction between product-specific advice and broad, unbiased financial-planning advice.
- The vast majority of advisers are compensated only if they sell a product. They don't make any money if they tell you to pay down debt, even if that's the best thing for you to do.
- As an owner-manager or professional, your circumstances are different. Most people preparing a financial plan for you won't take into account your unique circumstances or know enough about corporations to present good advice. For example, they will probably use average tax rates instead of your actual personal and corporate rates.

STEP FIVE

# 5 TALK

TO YOUR FAMILY

# NOW

Dinner was over and Gary was gathering up the plates to bring them into the kitchen. He was feeling good about seeing all four of his children together, something that rarely happened anymore.

It was Ashley's birthday, so tonight Carter and Melissa were back to join in the celebration. Of course, he still saw the older kids all the time, since both of them worked in the dealership. But there was something nice about the whole family — all six of them — being around the same table for a meal.

"Thanks everyone!" said Ashley cheerfully as she put on her coat.

"Where are you going?" said Gary.

"C'mon, Dad. You don't expect me to spend my 19th birthday in the house watching television, do you? I'm meeting Morgan and Samantha in 20 minutes."

"Have a good time," said Gary. "Remember —"

But there was no time for him to give her any safety reminders. No matter how cheerfully he intended to deliver them in order to avoid sounding like an overprotective dad, it was too late. She was already out the door.

Gary started putting the pots and pans in the sink.

"Why don't you leave that to me," said Jennifer. "I think the kids want to talk to you."

"Which kids?" Gary asked reflexively. Bobby had already disappeared to his room, which left just Carter and Melissa. He saw them every day at work. Why did they want to talk to him now? And since when did Jennifer offer to take over the dishes when he had already started on them? Was this some kind of set-up?

"Come and sit down for a second, Dad," said Melissa. Carter was already at the dining room table, looking a bit uncomfortable.

This was all starting to seem a bit serious.

Gary sat down at the table. "Is one of you pregnant or getting married?" he asked.

"I'm not pregnant," said Carter. "We just wanted to talk about a couple of things."

"And before you think I put them up to this," said Jennifer from the kitchen, "it was all their idea. I didn't say a word to them, and it has nothing to do with what we were talking about yesterday."

"What were you talking about yesterday?" asked Melissa.

"Never mind about that," said Gary. "What's going on?"

"We've been chatting," said Carter. "And we wanted to sit down with you..."

"And talk about some long-term planning for the business," said Melissa.

"We have some ideas," said Carter.

"And we just want to put them on the table," said Melissa.

"You guys are finishing each other's sentences," said Gary. "That's a bad sign." Although he was starting to think maybe it was more worrisome for him than it was for them. Clearly, a lot of thought had gone into this.

Melissa had expected the conversation to be difficult. She'd wanted to have it for more than a year, but Carter had always discouraged it. He didn't want to put any unnecessary pressure on his father. Instead, he told her they should wait for a better time, although that never seemed to materialize. Finally, something happened that forced his hand, and he had agreed to be part of the discussion, as long as she took the lead.

"So, come on," said Gary. "Out with it."

"Succession planning," Melissa blurted out. "We want to talk about succession planning."

"But not, like, immediate," Carter quickly added. "You know, in the future."

"Well I'm glad we're not talking about doing it retroactively," said Gary. "We're having a good year."

"Just hear them out," Jennifer piped in from the kitchen. Gary noticed that she was choosing when to run the tap strategically so that the sound didn't drown out any important parts of the conversation.

"I know you're still relatively young," said Melissa.

"Thank you for that," said Gary. "Especially for the word 'relatively'."

"And I know you're not planning to retire for a few more years."

"That's true."

"But there's nothing wrong with figuring out what we're going to do and how we're going to do it."

"Even if we don't know exactly when it's going to happen," said Carter.

"What's the hurry?" said Gary.

"You always said you would like us to take over someday," said Melissa. "I'm not saying we're ready yet, but I think we're ready to start having the conversation. There are people we can talk to who can help us through the process."

It was true — Gary had always told Carter and Melissa that he hoped one day they would be running the business. When they were kids, he used to bring them into the dealership on Saturdays, and they would watch TV in his office while he got some work done. But he would always say to them, "One day you'll be working here. One day this will be yours." He had said it very light-heartedly, of course; it was impossible to tell whether an eight-year-old and a six-year-old had what it took to run a car dealership. And he certainly didn't want to pressure them.

But since they were teenagers, both of them had worked at the dealership every summer, starting out by washing cars and doing administrative support. By the time they were in university, Melissa was working part-time in sales, and Carter was managing the service centre every summer while the regular managers were on holidays.

Gary encouraged them to try other jobs. He wouldn't have minded if they had worked in other careers first. While he found the idea of leaving the business to his kids satisfying and heart-warming, he wanted them to do it only if it were their choice. And as it turned out, they enjoyed the dealership so much that when they each graduated from university, they started working there full-time.

Last year, Melissa had become the business manager. And Carter was now one of the top sales representatives, outperforming some of the most experienced members of the team. They were doing well. But it was still too soon for them to take over. They weren't ready. More importantly, he wasn't ready.

"I'm proud of you guys," said Gary. "You're doing really well. But it's too soon to have this conversation. There's lots of time yet. For one thing, what if Ashley or Bobby wants to get involved as well? I don't want them to be left out."

"Ashley is studying kinesiology," said Melissa. "And Bobby wants to design smart phone apps. They haven't spent more than one summer each working in the dealership. They're not interested. We're there all the time."

"Nothing has changed," said Gary. "But I want to get the business to a certain level first. Then we can talk."

Melissa sighed. She was about to speak again but Carter beat her too it.

"Dad," he said. "We don't want to rush into anything either. We wouldn't feel comfortable taking over now. We just want to start planning for it. Other things can happen too, unexpected things."

"Like what? Me having a heart attack? Is that what you're saying?" Gary was starting to get a bit frustrated.

"No," said Carter.

"Yes, like you having a heart attack," said Melissa. "Exactly like that. What would we do? Have you ever thought about that?"

"I think about it all the time," said Gary.

"For God's sake, Dad, we're not kids anymore," said Melissa. She got up from the table. "Never mind. Forget we brought it up. See you tomorrow."

Gary sighed and watched as Melissa put on her coat.

"Good night, Dad," said Carter. He shrugged and smiled, trying to soften the tone a bit.

Gary watched the door close and walked into the kitchen.

"Before you say anything," he said, "what was I supposed to do? They're not ready yet."

"They're not ready or you're not ready?" said Jennifer.

"A bit of both, I guess."

"You're going to have to retire someday."

"It's not that I'm not ready to retire," said Gary. "I'm not ready to have the whole conversation about what happens next. It's too complicated. There's no way I can make everyone happy."

"We just need to figure out a way that's fair to everyone," said Jennifer.

"That's just it: I'm not sure if that exists. What about Ashley and Bobby? Not only that, what about us? Most of our money is tied up in the business. How will we get any of it out if we just let Melissa and Carter take over? Sometimes I think the best thing would be for me to sell it to someone else."

"What? How can you say that?"

"Well, then we could retire and whatever money we didn't need, we could split equally among the four kids."

"But you're talking about Melissa and Carter's futures, their dreams. I thought it was your dream, too."

"It was. But maybe that's all it ever was. Reality is a lot more complicated. I just don't want anyone to end up upset."

Jennifer kissed him on the cheek. "You can finish the dishes," she said.

This scenario is very familiar to us. We've seen countless businesses go through succession issues. No two situations are exactly the same, but there are some common themes:

- The owner or owners aren't ready to retire, for a variety of financial and emotional reasons.
- The children or other potential successors are impatient to play increasingly responsible roles in the business, and to see their

future plans solidified.

- Not everyone wants exactly the same thing to happen, or at least not on the same timetable. While that's not surprising, it's incredibly problematic.
- When family and business are mixed, conversations on the topic are emotional and awkward, sometimes turning into arguments. Or the subject is never broached because everyone wants to avoid the pain and aggravation of dealing with this tricky subject.
- There's an impulse to let inertia take over and to do and say nothing about the matter because it's complicated. And when families are involved, there's a risk of being preoccupied with treating children equally rather than fairly (there's a difference).

Succession planning is not easy, especially when it involves family dynamics. The situation that confronts many families is completely understandable. Even the parents who dream of retiring and handing off to their children want to do it at a time that's right for them and for the business. Nobody wants to feel like they're being pushed out the door.

And the tension over succession planning is hard to escape, since it involves the people you love most; in some cases, you share a home with them. Given the complexity of mixing business and family relationships, it shouldn't be surprising that this is a challenging process.

So families that are confronted with these challenges need to do two things.

First, they need to accept and acknowledge that they are not unusual. It may seem like other family businesses have smooth transitions from one generation to the next, but they probably don't. The vast majority of family businesses struggle with succession issues. For some, it gets so complicated that relationships are fractured, and in some cases loving family members end up not speaking to each other for weeks or months.

Second, they need to get help. In most cases, it's not realistic to expect to resolve the complex emotional and financial issues involved in a successful generational transition without some outside assistance.

Unfortunately, many families treat succession like a transaction rather than a process. They think it's like selling a property, just to someone within the family rather than an outside buyer. So they wait far too long to confront the issues, resolve tensions, and lay the groundwork for a successful transition. Succession planning is indeed a process, and it's one that needs to begin a long time before the actual transition takes place.

It doesn't matter whether the eventual transition is one that is internal, external, or involving family members. Our recommendation is to start the discussion as early as possible — at least five years before retirement — and to bring in outside help. A facilitated process allows everyone to speak openly and honestly about their feelings and objectives, without the fear that they will offend anyone or damage any of the important relationships in their lives.

Unfortunately, as human beings we don't like to confront uncomfortable topics. So we put them off, hoping the issues will go away. But retirement and succession planning don't go away; instead, they just get closer every day. So you need to fight the inertia.

For a business owner in this state of inertia, a fundamental paradigm shift is required. You have to move from seeing the transition as a threat to viewing it as an opportunity. After all, you probably always wanted to sell your business one day, or at least stop working as many hours. Now there's someone who could take over, and on terms that are favourable to you and take into account your needs. You should be happy about that. And with a little more information, a thoughtful and non-confrontational exchange of ideas, and a well-constructed plan, many of the scary aspects of transitions can be resolved and eliminated.

An experienced facilitator, with expertise in everything from behavioural sciences to financial matters, has the advantage of being outside the business or family, and impartial. Since everyone involved has a vested interest, no one individual can set aside his or her own personal stake and feelings to look at the bigger picture.

Without a proper process and an experienced facilitator, you're just going to have everyone arguing for their own position.

A facilitator will seek to align everyone's interests, so there's eventual consensus about what's best for everyone. It doesn't happen quickly, and the facilitator doesn't act alone. You should engage all of the existing players in your business and family, including lawyers, accountants, and other advisers, and perhaps even mentors and colleagues who understand the business.

So in Gary's case, if he's thinking of retiring in the next five to seven years, he shouldn't wait any longer to start exploring how the transition will take place. After all, even if he hands over control to his kids, they're going to want him to stick around for a while and help them. And clearly, since Melissa and Carter want to talk about it, there are risks to not beginning the dialogue. Let's put it this way: putting it off won't make it any better; indeed, it will likely make it much worse, leaving Gary in a situation where he might have to act urgently in response to a crisis, rather than in a careful, planned fashion.

There are many factors that affect the decisions around succession planning, so we can't prescribe one solution. But we can tell you that there's a process that works. It's not simple, but it is straightforward and effective. And many families have been through it, and have engineered successful transitions with minimal pain and aggravation.

We totally understand why so many business owners are reluctant to start the process. It's an uncomfortable topic and many people feel they are surrendering control if they even entertain the discussion. But it can be done and done well. And no matter how problematic it appears, a good process can result in a solution that works for everyone.

A successful transition planning process will take you from being afraid of the uncomfortable topic to being completely at ease with it, because you know the outcome will happen properly and meet everyone's needs.

# SUMMARY

Here are the key points you should remember about succession planning:

- Just as there's no such thing as a perfect family, a family business with a perfectly smooth generational transition does not exist.
- Succession planning is a process, not a transaction.
- There are no benefits and only risks to putting off the process. You should start discussing transition at least five years before it happens.
- Especially within families, transitions are financially and emotionally complex, so it's difficult to achieve everyone's goals without the help of an experienced facilitator with expertise in this area.

STEP SIX

# 6 HIRE A QUARTER-BACK

As they pulled out of the driveway, Mike glanced over at Sandra. "I'm just saying we should talk about it. We always said —"

"I know," said Sandra. "And I'm not ruling it out. Just give me time to think about it."

It was only a few weeks after their meeting at the bank, but until that morning, Mike had put his pursuit of a cottage on hold. The financial plan had not helped his case in any way. It had ended up on the dining room table, just like the last one. Mike hadn't bothered to throw it in the recycle bin yet, but they both knew it didn't meet their requirements. They had barely spoken about it since the meeting ended.

But that evening, as he and Katie set up the telescope on the back deck, Mike had been approached by his neighbour Peter Young. Peter and his wife Tara had moved in five years earlier, with kids about the same age as Katie and Jake, and the two families had become quite close. There were regular barbecues in the summer, and the four kids often ended up playing together at one house or the other.

Every summer, Peter and Tara had invited Mike and Sandra and their kids to their cottage for a week. It was in a great location, about 45 minutes from the city, on a quiet lake. It was exactly the kind of cottage Mike and Sandra had always dreamed of owning. Just last August, during a beautiful evening in front of the fire after the kids had gone to sleep, Sandra said to Tara, "If you ever hear of another cottage for sale in this area, you have to let us know."

Sandra meant it mostly as a way of telling Peter and Tara how lucky she thought they were. Besides, the lake was so popular that cottages were rarely put on the market. When someone wanted to sell, they usually had a friend or relative who wanted to buy, so you almost never saw properties listed with an agent.

A month ago, Peter and Tara had shared with Mike and Sandra some exciting news: they were expecting a third child. And that morning, Peter had told Mike that they were going to start looking for a bigger house. There just wasn't enough room for three children in their current home. And since a new house in the same neighbourhood would cost a lot of money, they had decided to put their cottage up for sale.

"Before we tell anyone else, though," said Peter, "we wanted to give you guys first crack at it. There's only one condition: you have to let us come visit once in a while."

Mike was astonished. It was the perfect cottage and they would be getting an exclusive opportunity to make an offer. It couldn't be better.

Even Sandra was tempted. Despite her apprehension about money, she wanted a cottage as much as Mike did. And she had to admit, Peter and Tara's place was ideal for their needs. It was close enough that Mike could stay up there with the kids for weeks at a time in the summer while she commuted back and forth to the clinic.

As they drove to the annual dinner at the golf club, Sandra was feeling very torn. On the one hand, she had been thinking that maybe Mike was right. Even that superficial plan from the bank had shown that they had good cash flow. Maybe they should just seize the moment and start living the life they'd always dreamed about. What's the worst that could happen?

On the other hand, Sandra was concerned about her parents. Her dad's health hadn't been ideal lately. Mike and Sandra were already supporting their living expenses every month. What if her father needed some additional care? That could be thousands of dollars a month. And she was the only one they could turn to for that kind of money.

When they parked at the club, Sandra turned to Mike. "Honey," she said. "I'm seriously considering the cottage. I really am. But I think we need to sort out a few things first just to make sure we can do it. We can do it quickly so we can give them an answer. I promise."

"Okay," said Mike. This was the closest she had come to agreeing to the cottage in months, so he wasn't going to argue.

"I think we should talk to a professional accountant," said Sandra. "One of my colleagues recommended someone — and it's not the same person who sent us to the bank. We need to get a proper plan done, and then we can decide about these things."

"Just think how much Katie will be able to see through the telescope when she doesn't have all the light from the city interfering."

"Okay, that's enough," said Sandra.

As Mike and Sandra walked to the door, they saw another couple walking towards them.

"Gary! Jennifer!" said Mike.

"Hello Mike," said Gary. "Hello Sandra."

The two couples embraced and started walking into the club together. They had already planned to sit at the same table for dinner, as they always did. Jennifer and Sandra went to sit down while Mike and Gary got drinks.

Mike quickly briefed Gary on the cottage development. "But don't bring it up at dinner," he said. "I don't want to put any pressure on Sandra."

"I won't," said Gary. "Besides, wait until you hear the day I've had," said Gary. They gathered up the drinks and went back to the table.

Jennifer and Sandra were smiling as they approached.

"So, Gary," said Sandra. "I hear you have a bit of a personnel issue you have to resolve."

"I guess you could call it that," said Gary.

"What's going on?" said Mike.

"Melissa came to see me today," said Gary.

"Is she pregnant?" said Mike.

"No!" Jennifer squealed. "She's most certainly not. I'm not ready to be a grandmother."

"She's been offered another job," said Gary. "A really good one. You know Jim Walker?"

"He owns a bunch of dealerships, right?"

"Right. He wants her to manage one of them."

"I thought Melissa and Carter were going to take over your business one day," said Mike.

"So did Melissa," said Jennifer. "But Gary's been stalling on that."

"I haven't been stalling," said Gary. "I'm just not ready yet."

"Sounds like stalling to me," said Mike. "Anyway, I guess you've got to make a decision now, don't you?"

"Yes, I do," said Gary. "I got in touch with a guy today, an accountant. He's worked with a couple of the other car dealers I know. I'm going to have to start on this whole succession planning thing. I don't have any choice now. We have a bunch of other things we need to sort out as well. I guess it's the right thing to do anyway."

"If it makes your daughter happy and keeps her working with you, I'd say it's definitely the right thing to do," said Sandra.

"I'm certainly not going to lose her to Jim Walker," said Gary.

Over the course of the past six sections, we've identified a number of areas of concern for Gary and Jennifer and Sandra and Mike. In each case, there is both significant financial risk and the potential for unnecessary anxiety and stress.

We'd like to tell you the solutions for both families are simple, but they aren't. There are many benefits to being an owner-manager or professional, but there are also unique circumstances that require a sophisticated approach. There's a proper and effective way to do things that will yield the right results, including peace of mind, but it's different for everyone.

So you need help determining and implementing the right approach. Like a professional athlete or entertainer, you need a team. For a pro golfer, that group might include an agent, a swing coach, a nutritionist, and other experts. In your case, it's a group of advisers to help you navigate issues like tax planning, insurance, succession planning, and more.

You may have some of that team in place already. You probably work with a lawyer and an accountant. You may even have an insurance broker and a financial adviser. Some of these individuals may be people you have known and worked with for a long time, people you trust with your affairs.

But is there someone who brings all the pieces together and ensures you have a plan that works for your circumstances, with nothing falling through the cracks? Who understands all the different aspects of your life and how they all fit together? Who sits down with you once a year to review your long-term plans, make sure everything is on track, and make the necessary adjustments to ensure your interests are protected?

You might think that person is you. But it shouldn't be. If you're trying to do it all yourself, you're like someone with no building experience and a full-time job deciding to be the general contractor for a brand-new home. You don't have the time or the expertise to do it properly.

Instead, you need someone to be the quarterback of your team. You need what we refer to as the trusted adviser.

The trusted adviser isn't like the other members of your team. He or she is the one person who has a thorough understanding of your needs and objectives, and is prepared to see them through. The trusted adviser is someone who acts on your behalf, not on behalf of an insurance or mutual fund company. He or she understands your goals and your unique circumstances, and doesn't apply a template or a cookie-cutter to them. The trusted adviser integrates all the pieces of your life, not just some of them, into one comprehensive financial plan, then makes sure you stay on track to achieve the results, without making any of the costly mistakes arising from the pitfalls that we've outlined in this book.

While you focus on your business or your practice, the trusted adviser makes sure you have a sophisticated, integrated approach. You don't pull the pieces together, he or she does. And the trusted adviser doesn't replace the existing advisers and experts in your life; he or she coordinates them and makes sure they are all working together to achieve your goals. For example, if your tax accountant is working side-by-side with your wealth manager, then it is much more likely that your capital gains will be timed to minimize your taxes.

Traditionally, there haven't been a lot of people who have worked in this space. But increasingly, it's becoming a niche for some experts who want to help owner-managers and professionals protect their own interests and achieve their long-term goals in a complex and often-tricky environment.

The trusted adviser is someone who sits down with you at least once a year to review your plan, discusses the tax issues faced by you, your family and your corporation, determines what factors and assumptions have changed, and revises and adjusts your plan accordingly.

Working with a trusted adviser saves you time and gives you peace of mind, because you don't have to be an expert in these areas yourself, nor do you have to implement all of the action items. Your trusted adviser will work with your lawyer, your accountant, and other advisers to make sure everything is aligned and gets done. It doesn't mean you won't still work with these other experts, especially those you trust; it just means that there will be someone who, like you, sees the bigger picture and, unlike you, has the time and expertise to act on it.

There are many criteria for choosing someone you can work with, including everything from credentials to chemistry. However, we can't stress this enough:

## YOUR TRUSTED ADVISER MUST BE SOMEONE WHO SPECIALIZES IN WORKING WITH OWNER–MANAGERS AND PROFESSIONALS.

You can't hire a pretender in this area. If your adviser doesn't have the experience and the expertise, it's you who will pay the price. You could end up wasting a lot of money on taxes and fees.

There are specialists who work primarily with wealthy people. There are others who have expertise at working with families or other individuals. But as an owner-manager or professional, you have many unique considerations that must be incorporated into your plans. Many of these considerations have serious financial implications if they are not handled correctly. You shouldn't expect to know everything about these areas yourself.

And it's crucial that you don't rely on advice from someone who is paid a commission to sell a product. That person isn't aligned with your interests.

To achieve your goals with minimal risk and maximum reward, you can't have someone who looks at only one side of the picture, or rely on a series of advisers who each looks at only one component of your affairs. Your trusted adviser should understand all the different facets of your life so that there will be no missed opportunities or wasted resources.

He or she should be someone who understands your business or your practice, and who works with others in your field. Your trusted adviser should be able to help you with your professional as well as your personal life, providing tax advice, business planning guidance, and more.

If you don't have a trusted adviser quarterbacking your affairs, you're counting on yourself to make sure all the pieces of your financial life fit together properly. That's not realistic. Remember: you're an expert at what you do. Your clients or patients trust your expertise and advice. You should do the same when it comes to your financial affairs.

## SUMMARY:

Here are the key points you should remember about choosing and working with a trusted adviser:

- As a business owner or professional, you don't have the time and expertise to coordinate all the aspects of your financial affairs.
- You need a quarterback, a trusted adviser, who pulls together

all the different facets of your life into one financial plan and series of actions, including working with your existing advisers and ensuring that nothing falls through the cracks.

- Your trusted adviser must have expertise and experience in working with owner-managers and professionals.
- Your professional accountant may be the only one of your current advisers who combines all the necessary skills and experience to fulfill the role of trusted adviser. Ideally, you should try to find a firm that can provide not only tax and accounting skills, but also financial planning and wealth management expertise as well.

# EPILOGUE

As the headlights appeared at the end of the long lane, Mike walked to the corner of the deck.

"They're here!" he shouted.

"Just in time for the campfire," Sandra answered from the kitchen. Katie and Jake came running from the other side of the cottage. It was past their bedtime, but with visitors expected, they wouldn't be able to fall asleep anyway.

The sleek SUV pulled up to the cottage. Jennifer opened the door with a bottle of wine, a box of pastries in her hands and a sheepish grin on her face. "Sorry we got here so late," she said.

"That's okay," said Mike. "There's no rush. Nice wheels, Gary."

"Brand new," said Gary. "Next year's model just arrived at the dealership this week."

"The dealership?" said Mike. "I thought you never went there anymore."

"Uncle Gary," said Katie. "I want to show you something in my telescope."

"How's that telescope working out?" asked Jennifer. "It's been almost a year that you've had that, isn't it?"

"She loves it," said Sandra. "Here, let's get your stuff inside." She and Jennifer went into the cottage while Gary and Mike followed Katie and Jake around back.

"And how is life at Majestic Lake," asked Gary, "at the cottage that was never to be?"

"Fantastic," said Mike. "I've been up here all week with the kids. Sandra arrived tonight. We don't go back until Tuesday."

"How did you convince Sandra to go for it?"

"Oh, I have my ways," said Mike. "How was Florida?"

"Hot," said Gary. "I'm still getting used to being there in the summer. But it's great. We just got back on Wednesday."

"You were there three weeks this time?"

"Yep."

"No withdrawal? No attachment issues, being away from the dealership that long?"

"Not really. They send me regular updates. And I can check the numbers online anytime I want."

"I'll just get everything set up," said Katie.

In the kitchen, Sandra opened the bottle and poured Jennifer a glass. "Three straight weeks in Florida. How did you get Gary to go along with that?"

"He's feeling a lot better about leaving Melissa and Carter in charge. He's learning to let go."

"That's a big change," said Sandra.

"Well, he still checks the sales numbers three times a day. He doesn't think I notice."

Sandra laughed.

"The process we've been going through has been great," says Jennifer. "We're not all the way there yet, but everybody is still on speaking terms. The whole family meets every two weeks to move things forward."

"All of you?"

"Yep, all of us. It's really quite fascinating, actually. We're all talking to each other like grown-ups. It's kind of hilarious in a way. But very productive."

"I can't imagine Jake speaking to me like a grown-up," said Sandra. "Someday, I guess."

"All these other things are happening too. Melissa is taking these great courses right now. And she does one-on-one training with Gary for a few hours every week. At least, when we're not in Florida."

"Wow," said Sandra.

"Now, how about you?" said Jennifer. "Look at this place. And you, here on a Friday night. Are you feeling okay about everything?"

"I'm trying to be Happy-Go-Sandra!"

"Seriously, though, you're good with it all? I remember when this would have caused a lot of sleepless nights."

"Actually, yes. We've been working with this team of accountants, and it turns out I don't have to save ever single cent I earn. I can relax and enjoy life a bit. Not that I've admitted any of this to Mike. He thinks he's just very persuasive."

"Ha!" said Jennifer. "Always good to let them think it's their idea."

"But it's been really interesting. We have a plan now. You have no idea how much difference that makes."

"I do, actually," said Jennifer.

"It's funny," said Sandra. "Last weekend, Katie was showing me something through the telescope, and it kind of struck me."

"How small our little planet is and how all the things we worry about are basically meaningless?" said Jennifer.

"No," said Sandra, laughing. "Well, sort of. It just gave me a bit of perspective that when you've got a good balance to everything and you can get a clear view of how things look from far away, you don't worry as much about the small details."

"Hmm," said Jennifer. "I think I know what you mean."

"You just get a feeling that you're on the right course and you can relax and enjoy it a little bit because everything is falling into place as it should."

They walked outside with their wine glasses to join the others.

"And how's the stock portfolio, Gary?" asked Mike. "Still bouncing up and down like a bungee jumper?"

"I don't actually know," said Gary. "I don't check it as often as I used to. Ever since we talked to that accountant and he put us into this new strategy, I don't really pay attention. They update me every once in a while."

"That sounds so, I don't know, healthy," said Mike. "I'm not sure I recognize you."

"Look right through there, Uncle Gary."

"What am I looking at, Katie?"

"It's Polaris. It's the north star."

"What was it again, Mike? The Small Lion or something?"

"The Little Bear, silly," said Katie.

"We have to get out to the golf course next week," said Gary. "I want to get a couple of rounds in while I'm in town."

"No problem. Happy to beat you anytime," said Mike.

"Be careful, Mike," said Jennifer. "Gary's game is getting a bit better. He's been playing a lot in Florida."

"You should have seen the putt I made this week," said Gary. "Even you would have been impressed."

Jennifer put a hand on Katie's shoulder. "Let me have a look," she said. "Your mom tells me the view is amazing."

# ACKNOWLEDGEMENTS

We would like to express our appreciation for Mark Sutcliffe's insightful direction and unwavering support. Without his diplomatic steering, this book would have become too much like another textbook. The number of his creative ideas that ended up in this book is too high to count. Thank you, Mark, for helping us to turn this book into something people might not only find useful but also enjoy reading.

We would like to thank everyone who helped with this project including Doug Black, Steve Doty, Sue Fagnan, Gord Hardie, Lynn Honsberger, Wayne Leckie, Luke MacLennan, Joe Schlett, Martha Skeggs, Carol Vahey and Barbara van Moorsel.

We would also like to remember the late Peter Hoysted for his vision and enthusiasm and for encouraging the two of us to start working together.

Doug McLarty & Ross McShane
September 2013

# ABOUT THE AUTHORS

**J. DOUGLAS McLARTY** FCPA, FCA, CFP, TEP

MANAGING DIRECTOR

MCLARTY & CO PROFESSIONAL CORPORATION

A true entrepreneur in his own right, Doug McLarty is the founder and managing director of McLarty & Co. At the heart of Doug's success is his desire to be more than his clients' accountant. Doug enjoys drawing on his 30 years of experience when working with clients on strategic planning issues and in developing and integrating personal financial plans with innovative business plans. Among the firm's clients are more than 200 health-care professionals and more than two dozen car dealerships. McLarty & Co also has substantial internal expertise in the real estate and construction industries.

To meet more of its clients' needs "under one roof," McLarty & Co added new lines of business to its traditional accounting, assurance and tax services. In 2009 Ross McShane brought his financial planning and wealth management expertise to the company. In 2010 Doug became an accredited succession planning adviser with SuccessCare®. Cross-border taxation services were added when Martha Skeggs joined the team in early 2011. McLarty & Co is the only public accounting company in Ottawa to offer such an extensive set of financial services.

Doug is well-known in Ottawa as a business and community leader. He cofounded the Ottawa Business Network and is a past chair of the Riverside Hospital. In 2000, the Institute of Chartered Accountants of Ontario (ICAO) recognized Doug's contribution to the community and his profession by awarding him fellowship status. Doug currently volunteers with the ICAO in communications and lobbying capacities. He also serves on the board of directors of Ottawa Hydro and is the chair of the board of the Independent Accountants' Financial Group.

Carleton University, McGill University and the ICAO have all engaged Doug as a lecturer. Local and national media have published Doug's articles, and interviewed and quoted him on a variety of taxation and financial planning topics.

*"At McLarty & Co, we think of ourselves as key players on your team, quarterbacking your personal and business financial game plans, freeing you to do what you do best."*

**ROSS McSHANE** CGA, CFP, RFP, CIM

DIRECTOR OF FINANCIAL PLANNING SERVICES

MCLARTY & CO WEALTH MANAGEMENT

CORPORATION

Drawing on more than 30 years of experience in the financial services industry, Ross McShane provides meaningful financial planning services that integrate personal and corporate taxation, estate planning, insurance, and wealth management. His financial plans are working documents that he reviews and updates regularly so they don't become outdated or end up sitting on a shelf.

A recognized expert in his field, Ross is regularly published and quoted in the national media on financial-planning issues. He contributes his financial planning and tax advice to the *Globe and Mail, Canadian MoneySaver,* and *MoneySense,* and has been interviewed on national television and local radio.

Ross's excellent financial planning skills were recognized by the Independent Accountants' Investment Counsel (IAIC), which named him Financial Advisor of the Year, and named McLarty & Co Wealth Management Corporation their Wealth Management Firm of the Year.

Ross graduated from the University of New Brunswick with a Bachelor of Business Administration and holds the Certified General Accountant, Certified Financial Planner, Registered Financial Planner, and Chartered Investment Manager designations. He is also licensed to sell insurance products and advise clients on insurance matters and products in Ontario.

*"There is no greater satisfaction than working with clients over a number of years and seeing them achieve their goals."*

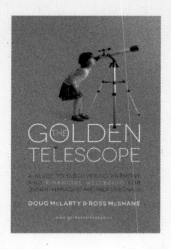

**DO YOU KNOW SOMEBODY WHO COULD BENEFIT FROM READING THE GOLDEN TELESCOPE? IT IS THE PERFECT GIFT FOR BUSINESS OWNERS AND HEALTH PROFESSIONALS.**

You can order it online at www.goldentelescope.ca or you can mail, fax or scan this order form to us.

| | | | |
|---|---|---|---|
| **Number of copies:** _____ | | **Method of payment:** | |
| Price per copy* $19.95 | | ☐ Enclose or send a cheque payable to McLarty & Co Professional Corporation. | |
| SUBTOTAL _____ | | | |
| HST (5%) _____ | | ☐ Call (613) 726.1010 with your credit card information. | |
| **TOTAL** _____ | | | |

*We offer a discount on orders of ten or more copies. Please contact us at info@mclartyco.ca.

Name: _____

Mailing Address: _____

City: _____

Province: _____ Postal Code: _____

Telephone: _____

Email: _____

**MAIL, FAX OR SCAN:**
McLarty & Co
110-495 Richmond Road, Ottawa, ON  K2A 4B2
Fax: (613) 726.9009  info@mclartyco.ca